Lefton China

Ruth McCarthy

Schiffer Publishing Ltd

Dedication

This book is dedicated to:

My husband, children, and grandchildren who have given me so much love and encouragement during this project, and to my grandson, Richard Bruce (Osborn) Ratliff. Know that you are thought of, missed, and loved, always.

My mother, Dorothy Virginia Ernest, with loving memories, who passed away July 23, 1994, at the age of 87. She loved beautiful china, and among her small collection were four pieces that started my extensive Lefton China collection. May she know what her small find did for my life!

To all the many, many Lefton collectors out there who have supported me in this venture. May you enjoy this book and find it useful in your collecting adventures. Don't ever give up looking for that extra special piece. It's out there somewhere waiting for you to find it!

Copyright © 1998 by Ruth McCarthy
Library of Congress Catalog Card Number: 97-80252

Book Design by Laurie A. Smucker

ISBN: 0-7643-0415-1
Printed in United States
1 2 3 4

Published by Schiffer Publishing Ltd.
4880 Lower Valley Road
Atglen, PA 19310
Phone: (610) 593-1777; Fax: (610) 593-2002
E-mail: schifferbk@aol.com
Please write for a free catalog.
This book may be purchased from the publisher.
Please include $3.95 for shipping.
Try your bookstore first.

We are interested in hearing from authors with book ideas on related subjects.

Contents

Acknowledgments

A heartfelt thank you, with love, to the following people:

My husband Dan McCarthy, for taking all the beautiful pictures. I could not have finished this book without his help, love, support, and patience. I found I was not the best photographer in the world and when I got discouraged he took over with a new camera, spending many hours taking pictures and talking with our developer.

Our children, Ray, Lee, Kathy, Debbie, Patti, Dawn, and Erin and their spouses. Our grandchildren, Jessica, Kyle, Nicole, Matthew, Heather, Michael, McKenna, Joe, Stephanie, Scott, Bruce, and Bryce, all of whom, I am sure, at times felt forsaken by Dan and I both during this past year!

Mike and Cindy Schneider, who said "You can," when I said "I can't." Their gentle push, support, help, and en-couragement allowed me to begin this book and they unselfishly supplied pictures and information from their own personal collection.

My friends, Vickie Colish, Linda Stutzman, and Sabra Cummins who went out of their way to find pieces of Lefton for my collection and book. Margaret Martin, who has been a lifetime friend and helped me get my start in the antique world and Lefton collecting. Sherry and Steve Sberna, who more than once surprised me with delightful Lefton pieces, as did Vicki Nitecki, Irene Michul, Tom Jarrett, and Mary and Don Yontz, to name just a few.

Fran Harris and Steve Bellamy at Snap Shots Inc. in Sandusky, Ohio, who worked with us closely and developed the photographs for this book.

Introduction

Almost everyone today has a collection of some kind. Whether it's two pieces or a thousand, cookie jars or Civil War items, collecting is exciting and addicting. It can also be expensive, but certainly doesn't have to be. Flea markets, garage sales, and dimly lit basements of antique malls still—and hopefully always will—have bargains for the collector and dealer.

My first serious collection was (and still is), gravy boats, or as some people call them, sauce dishes with under plates. My second serious collection started three years ago, after my mother passed away. She had four pieces of Lefton China and they were left to me. There was a bloomer girl, an angel, a vase, and a planter and they all had red stickers and strange letters and numbers on the bottom of them. Something happened to me after these precious pieces came into my hands. I fell in love and became addicted at the same time. For awhile, that's all I looked for. I stopped shopping for items to resell in my antique shop and had little interest in anything other than Lefton. In a very short time I collected more than six hundred pieces.

The best part about collecting is the challenge of looking for and finding that one special piece and the heart-pounding thrill you get when you see that piece you've been looking for. You know, the one that's part of a set, or the rare piece, or that one with the unusual mark or sticker. There it is peeking out of a dirty old box, on a shelf behind other items or right there in front of you and you wonder why no one else saw it. But no, they didn't, you did and now it's yours, to buy, take home, and cherish.

I enjoy a collection that can be used, and mine certainly is! Figurines and wall hangings are in every room of the house, banks collect coins, animals are used in groupings in china cabinets or on small table tops, and angels are on bathroom shelves and bedroom window sills. Most of my planters and vases contain plants from real to fake, ivy to tulips. Picture frames contain pictures, candle holders grip candles, most salt and pepper shakers are loaded and ready. Cookie jars sometimes contain what they were made for, but most often have in them those small bits of things one doesn't know where else to put. Several sets of canisters are packed away for future use, as a change every few months is nice and the canisters made by Lefton go with most any color scheme.

Everyday use and wear has made it almost impossible to find whole sets of dinner ware, at least in my area of the world. The teapots, coffee pots, sugars, creamers, and snack sets were normally used only occasionally, therefore they have survived longer, as did shelf items such as figurines, covered dishes, planters, and vases. I have only once found a complete set of anything that I was searching for, in one place. Finding that Brown Heritage teapot in one shop and, after a year or more of searching, finally finding the matching sugar and creamer, was such an excitement! The hardest pieces to find, in my search, were all the bloomer girls of one series, all in perfect condition. They, like many other Lefton pieces, are very fragile and easily chipped. I searched for three years for the final girl of a series before going into an Antique Mall and, lo and behold, there was the whole, complete set on one shelf! After thinking this over, I have decided that finding one piece at a time is much more fun and challenging. It has given me the opportunity to find many other sought-after pieces that I may not have found.

I took my five-year-old granddaughter, Nicole, to Gallion, Ohio, on a Lefton hunt last summer and she was just starting to acquaint herself with the markings of Lefton. As with all beginning Lefton collectors, we were turning each piece over and checking the bottom mark. Several times she cried out, "Look Grandma, is this Lefton?" But it wasn't. Then she said, "Look Grandma, this is Lefton." Barely glancing at the piece I said, "No, that's not Lefton." She had this strange look on her face and insisted, "But it says it is!" So I looked a little closer and sure enough it was. It wasn't a piece I would have looked twice at so I would have missed it. Who was teaching who?

The list of items that the Lefton China Company has on the secondary market today seems endless. Pieces are made of bisque, an unglazed earthenware or porcelain that has been fired only once; matte, which is a flat finish, not glossy; porcelain, a shiny, high-gloss ceramic ware; milk china, a milk-white opaque glass, and hand-blown glass.

Flowers include Forget-me-not, Magnolia, Lily of the Valley, Rustic and Pink Daisy, Cosmos, Blue Astor, and Poppy. Types of roses include Misty, French, Moss, Blue, Tiffany, Americana, and Heirloom. And lets not forget Poinsettia, Holly Berry, Green Holly, Hot Poppy, Green Orchard, Golden Tree, Dogwood, and Brown and Green Heritage floral.

Chintz includes rose, blue, violet, and lilac. In Paisley there is rose, blue, and Fantazia. Among the fruit designs we find Green Orchard, Green Heritage, Brown Heritage, Pear 'N Apple, Grape, Fiesta (apple, pear, grapes, and cherries), Festival (grapes and leaves), and there may be more that I'm not aware of.

There are whimsical pieces such as Miss Priss, Blue Bird, Dainty Miss, Mr. Toodles, the little Dutch Girl, and the Cabbage Cuties, along with Elves, Pixies and Cupids to name a few, as well as several series of both Bloomer Girls and Angels that are highly sought after by collectors.

There are Lefton collectors throughout the country who want to buy, sell, or trade pieces and the quarterly newsletter on Lefton China is an excellent way to do this. You can join the National Society of Lefton Collectors by simply writing to the National Society of Lefton Collectors, 1101 Polk Street, Bedford, Iowa 50833, or by calling 712-523-2289. This newsletter is very informative, with updated news and pictures on the Lefton world, a classified section, personal stories, and much more.

Opposite right:
This Lefton advertising page was taken from *The Antiques Dealer* magazine, dated August, 1954. Published by Rosenthal and Smythe, Inc., it was a monthly publication circulated to dealers and devoted to their interests. This gives us dating information on pieces found on this page.

Opposite far right:
This Lefton advertising page was taken from *The Antiques Dealer* magazine, dated December, 1954. Published by Rosenthal and Smythe, Inc., it was a monthly publication circulated to dealers.

History

The Lefton China Company was founded in1941 by George Zoltan Lefton in Chicago, Illinois, and is still operating there today. Mr. Lefton was born in Hungary and made his living there by designing and manufacturing sportswear. His hobby while in Hungary was collecting fine china. After coming to the United States in 1939, he began shaping ideas for his own ceramic business. He began importing ceramic giftware from Asia after World War II. Although Japan has always been the major place of manufacture for Lefton China, starting in the 1970s manufacturing was expanded to other countries such as China, Taiwan, and Malaysia, to name but a few. Italy and England are also producing Lefton China, as can be seen by many of the pieces on the market today. The company is a wholesale business and their products can be found in retail gift shops all over the country. Due to the excellent quality, wide variety of styles, patterns, series, and themes, Lefton China will be in great demand for many years to come.

On May 29, 1996, Mr. George Zolton Lefton passed away at his winter home in Florida. He will be greatly missed by his family, friends, and Lefton collectors. Mr. Lefton has brought so much joy to many, many people who love and collect his fine china and will be remembered far into the future.

Mike Schneider wrote of Mr. Lefton and his legacy in *The Complete Cookie Jar* book:

"In recent years some import companies, Enesco for example, have considerably upgraded the quality of their ceramics to the point where there is little doubt they will become the collectibles of tomorrow. Lefton hasn't because there was no need to!"

What a fine tribute that was to George Zolton Lefton and the Lefton China Company.

Identifying Marks

Fired on trademarks (hereafter referred to as "stamps"), stickers/paper labels (large red, standard/medium red or black, small red, or orange) and numbers, are all identifying marks usually found on Lefton China. Letters preceding the numbers are the factory's abbreviated identification codes, and suffix letters may mean a variety of things such as right, left, the color of the item, small or large, to name just a few. Some pieces have the year of copyright on them and any or all of these trademarks are usually found on the bottom of the piece and aid in dating and identifying. Between 1945 and 1953, the pieces were merely stamped "Made in Occupied Japan," which makes it difficult to recognize the piece without consulting the brochures and catalogs put out by the Lefton China Company at that time.

In this book I have mentioned all the identifying marks found on each piece. The majority of items were made in Japan during the '50s, '60s, and '70s. Considering that many different and unusual markings have been found, I wanted to share them all. I was surprised by the find of a black sticker. Out of several hundred pieces, my collection has only four with this black sticker, and these are on Christmas items.

The mark "Limited Edition" is just that—very limited! The Blue Boy and Pinkie figurines in my collection are the only pieces I have ever seen that specifically say "Limited Edition." Surely there must be more, though I am not aware of what they are.

While searching for Lefton, pieces have been found with one, all, and none of these identifying marks. So how would you know if a piece is really Lefton if there are no marks to be found on it? There will be times when you won't know for certain. Paper labels are easily washed or worn off and have even been known to be lifted off and attached to items that are not Lefton. Therefore I check very closely with the paper labels. I have found pieces that have no markings but they have been part of a set or part of my existing collection and can be identified by that alone. There are identical pieces, but with different numbers or identical numbers on different pieces. Some have different factory codes, but the same number. Difficult? Sometimes yes. This is all part of the exciting challenge of finding Lefton.

I saw a beautiful piece not long ago while on route to South Carolina. It was a light pastel green bisque with cherubs. The marking on the piece simply said "Occupied Japan, Hand Painted." I believe this to be an older and perhaps rarer piece of Lefton, but the price was over $300. Did I want to pay that price for a piece that may not be Lefton? I wanted to do a little more research first. Several months later I went back to this shop and the piece was still there in the same place. However, this time the price had been raised $50, some of the leaves and flowers had been damaged, and the price tag said "Lefton perhaps?"

The dates for the following stickers/paper labels were derived from the first Lefton books written by Loretta DeLosier. Dating on a variety of the fired-on stamps used on Lefton will be found throughout this book.

The largest of the red stickers, with a silver or gold trim, was used from 1946-1953.

Standard or medium-size red stickers mainly had gold trim, although I have found some pieces with silver trim such as the one pictured here, used from 1953-1971.

Red stickers with gold trim like this were used in standard or medium-size from 1960-1983.

These red stickers with gold trim were used in standard or medium-size from 1962-1990.

Small red or orange stickers with gold trim came from Taiwan.

These standard or medium-size black stickers with a larger border of gold trim may have been used during the same time frame as the red sticker with same lettering, 1960-1983.

Pricing

Pricing, I believe, is the most difficult task of any collectibles book author. I have done a lot of research on this, comparing prices at auctions, antique shops, flea markets, private collectors, and dealers. Working in an antique mall has given me a chance to talk to people from all over the United States. I have never hesitated to talk to a customer about prices in their area. Some say there is a big difference, others say there is little to none. I have had extra Lefton pieces for sale in my shop and have listened to remarks from "Oh, look how reasonable this is," to "This is so high priced."

The majority of my buying has been done in flea markets and small, off-the-beaten-path antique stores between Ohio and South Carolina. I have found that prices vary greatly, depending on who's selling the items and where they are being sold. For example. In the basement of a small antique shop (basements are known to house items of little value) I found on the floor, in a dirty old box, the mushroom forest tureen. It was covered with dirt and cobwebs and had a 50-cent price tag. After cleaning it, much to my amazement, there was not a chip or crack to be found. Even the ladle was in perfect condition.

Another exciting find was a bloomer girl in the original box, covered with dust and laying on a floor in a flea market. The box was dirty but on inspection the little girl was wrapped and in perfect condition. This was a 25 cent item! On the other side of this coin, I have been known to pay twice the amount of any "book value" for a piece I really want or need to complete a series or set.

Please keep in mind that my intent is not to set prices for Lefton China! Prices are to be used as a guideline and not as gospel. The prices contained throughout this book are retail and for pieces in mint condition. Expect the price to be much lower for a damaged item and, unless you need the piece to complete a collection or it is extremely rare, think twice before buying it. A damaged piece is usually of little value to the collector or the dealer.

Photos

Animals

From tiny mice to large elephants, domestic to wild, Lefton has created them in fine porcelain, matte, or bisque. They are exquisitely hand painted or decorated with stones, flowers, glass eyes, and spaghetti type fur. The cow series is truly unique!

There are so many things you can do to liven up a collection of animals. By using bails of straw or hay, small barns, fences, gravel, buckets, trees, and flowers you turn plain animals on a shelf into real conversation pieces.

Cats

Siamese mother and kitten. 5" & 3.5". #H4039 & #H4032. $40-45 pair.

Siamese kittens, different poses, 3", #1562, stickers. $10-12 each.

Marks on kitten #H4032. Sticker used 1962-1990.

Marks on kittens #1562. Sticker used 1953-1971.

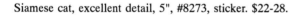

Siamese cat, excellent detail, 5", #8273, sticker. $22-28.

Marks on kitten #07593. Taiwan, 1990.

Kitten, 3.25", Birthstone, August Peridot, #07593, signed, stamp and sticker. She has a heart bracelet with the birthstone around her neck. $15-18.

Mother and kitten, black, gray, and white, 6", #5639, sticker. $20-25 pair.

This kitten has a lot of red color in the fur, 3.5", sticker. $10-12.

Mother and kitten with white fur, 5.5" and 3.5", #H1513 and #H1514. $18-20 for mom, $10-12 kitten.

Mother and two kittens, 5.5" and 3.5", #1513, #1514, and #1515. Different coloring and poses than #H1513 and #H1514. $18-20 for mom, $10-12 for kitten.

Two playful kittens, different poses, 3" long, sticker. These are pink porcelain. $25-28 pair.

Small brown kitten with butterfly and bow, 2.5", #150, sticker. $10-12.

Brown and white cat with red tones in fur, 5.5", #H2922, stamp. (*Courtesy of Mike and Cindy Schneider*) $15-18.

Cat with red tones in fur, 4.25", #H6364, stamp, sticker. (*Courtesy of Mike and Cindy Schneider*) $12-15.

Kitten with dark brown stripes and red tones in fur, 4.75", #H5364, stamp. (*Courtesy of Mike and Cindy Schneider*) $12-15.

Dogs

Small white poodle, 3.5", sticker. $15-18.

Standing white poodle, 5.5", sticker. $18-22.

Large black poodle, 5", sticker. $25-30.

White poodle puppies with adorable expressions! 3" and 4", #613, sticker. $15-18 each.

White fancy fur poodle, 5", #H1954, sticker. $25-30.

White poodles with spaghetti-type fur, mom with two babies, together with chains, #80204, sticker. $40-45.

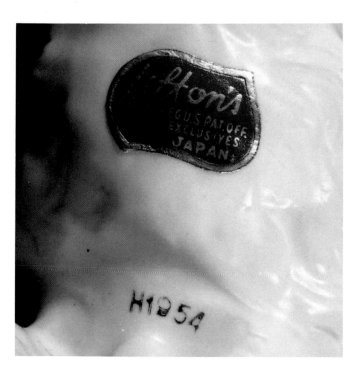

Pink poodles with spaghetti-type fur, mom with one baby. (Should be two). #885. $40-45 with two babies.

Marks on Poodle #H1954. Stamp used 1953-1971.

16

Pair of white poodles with large eyes, sticker, 4". $12-15 each.

Three-piece set of white poodles with pink bows, gold trim, and spaghetti fur. 6.5", 4.5", and 3.25", large red sticker. $85-90 for all three.

Little white poodle with collar and box, 3", #164, sticker. $10-12.

German shepherd, #H7326, sticker, 5", $35-40.

Marks on German shepherd #H7326. Sticker used 1960-1983.

Collie, #H7328, sticker, 5". $35-40.

"English Bull Dog" stamped on bottom, sticker, #2563, 4" by 6". $45-50.

"Wired Hair terrior" stamped on bottom, sticker, 5.5" by 6". $38-42.

"Champion Bassett Hound" on tag around neck, #8214, sticker 4". $40-45.

The detail is remarkable on this large beagle puppy, 7.5", # H8165. $35-40.

Marks on beagle puppy. Sticker used 1962-1990.

"St. Bernard" stamped on bottom, sticker, 5.5". $40-45.

Marks on German shepherd. Sticker used 1953-1971.

German shepherd and puppy, 5.5". $35-40.

Large 9" collie, sticker. $40-45.

Brown, black, and white boxer puppies in a basket, #H3710, 3". $18-22.

Black and white cocker spaniel puppies in a basket. They look like they are begging to be taken home! #H3710, 3". $20-23.

"Schnauzer" stamped on bottom of this puppy, sticker, 4.5. $18-22.

Four tiny puppies, Series #06329, stickers, 2.5". $15-20 each.

Two long-haired terrier puppies, #9051 & #C9051, stickers, 3". $12-15 each.

Puppy with a gun and duck, bisque, #00325, stamp, 3.5". $15-18.

Two puppies with bows around their necks, #1563, sticker, 2.5" and 3". $10-12 each.

These three puppies have "spaghetti" ears and tails, with bees on their heads, stickers, 3" and 4". $55-60.

Large German shepherd, 9.5", sticker. (*Courtesy of Mike and Cindy Schneider*) $50-55.

Boston Terrier, 5.5", #80521, stamp, sticker. (*Courtesy of Mike and Cindy Schneider*) $30-35.

Dog with a horn and hat, matte finish, #2731, sticker, 4". $18-20.

Chihuahua, 5.5", #H7328, stamp. (*Courtesy of Mike and Cindy Schneider*) $30-35.

Miscellaneous Animals

Scottie dog, 3.5", #691, sticker. $20-25.

These five cows have a description sticker on their sides and all are 6.5" long with excellent detailing. This is the Holstein cow, #446, red sticker. $50-60.

Black angus cow, #445, sticker. $50-60.

Jersey cow, #448, sticker. $50-60.

Ayrshire cow,#449, sticker. $50-60.

Black angus bull, #447, sticker. $50-60.

Chipmunk holding nut, 3.5", #03434, sticker. $12-15.

Skunk holding flower, 3.5", #7695, sticker, stamp. $12-15.

Brown rabbit with dark brown eyes, 4", #A6661, stamp. $15-18.

Panda, 3.5", #03434, sticker. $12-15.

White bunny with pink eyes, 4", #H880. $15-18.

White bunnies with pink eyes, 4.5" and 2", #H7143, 1974, stickers. $20-25 pair.

Cute white bunny, appears to be laughing, 4", sticker. $15-18.

Adorable little mice, one is reading, the other sweeping, 2.5", #00303, stamp, stickers. $10-12 each.

Squirrel with nuts, 5", #KW4749, stamp. $35-40.

Funny bunny with basket of flowers and a bird on her head, 4", #2721, stamp, sticker. $15-18.

Chipmunk eating nuts, bisque, 5.5", #KW4748, stamp. $35-40.

White sheep with bell and flowers around neck, 3", #06064, sticker. $12-15.

Pair of baby white lambs, 3" and 4", #H4546, stickers. $10-12 each.

Lamb, cute expression on face, 4.5", #3102, sticker. $18-20.

Pair of Irish pigs. 2.25", stickers. $15-18 pair.

Elephant, 10.5" x 12", #H5069, sticker. (*Courtesy of Jane Fuller*) $85-90.

Three elephants, 3.5", #H2673, 4", # H2674, 5.5", #H2675, all have stickers. (*Courtesy of Jane Fuller*) $20-25, $25-30, and $30-35.

Black and white horse, 4.5", #1350, Japan, sticker. $25-30.

Adorable mother chimp and baby, 4.5", #5669, sticker. $40-45.

Marks on horse #1350. Sticker used 1960-1983.

All-white horse with black hoofs, 4", #857, sticker. $25-30.

Tan and white colt, 4", #H547, sticker. $25-30.

White colt with black hoofs, 4.5", #1811, sticker. $20-25.

Tiger cub, 3.5", #H6658, $15-18. (*Courtesy of Kathy Osborn*)

Marks used on tiger cub #H6658. Sticker used 1960-1983.

Lion cub, 3.5", #H7061, $15-18. (*Courtesy of Kathy Osborn*)

Jaguar, 8" long, #9032, sticker. $60-65.

Lion, 3", #H7063, sticker. $18-20. (*Courtesy of Robin Goodsite*)

Pink porcelain deer with spaghetti trim, gold applied bow and rhinestone inset eyes, 7.5", large red sticker. $50-55.

Little 4" pink pig with spaghetti hair and stone insets, #6518, sticker. $18-22.

Banks

The whimsical children and animal banks made by Lefton are just the thing to get children to save some of their hard-earned allowance! There are so many to choose from. Need to save a few dollars for those upcoming summer garage sales? The Pin Money banks are good for that. Sure beats the old sock filled with quarters in a drawer.

Mom and baby kangaroo bank, porcelain., 8", #A2778, sticker. $35-40.

Tiger bank, 6", porcelain, #H6837, sticker. $20-25.

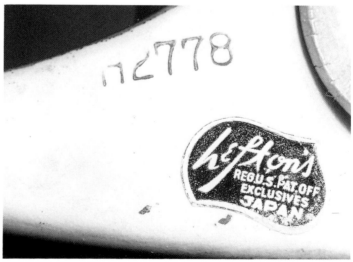

Marks on kangaroo bank #A2778. Sticker used 1953-1971.

Adorable pink piggy bank, 5", #03663, porcelain, beautiful color and detail. $30-35.

Mouse bank, light gray with glass eyes, porcelain, 6", #H3833R. $20-25.

Marks on pink piggy bank #03663. Korea sticker.

Dark gray mouse bank with glass eyes, porcelain, 5", #H4302, "Japan," sticker. $18-22.

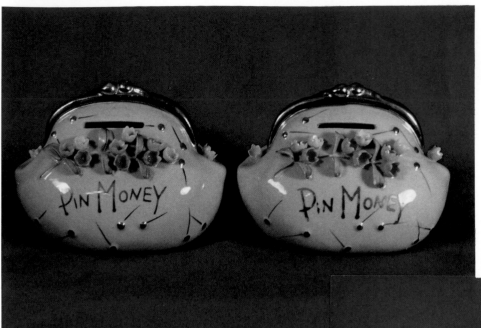

"Pin Money" bank, 4", stamped, porcelain. $40-45 each.

"Pin Money" bank, 5", porcelain, #90250, sticker. $40-45.

Marks on bank #90250. Sticker used 1953-1971.

Grandpa "Retirement Fund" banks, porcelain, two sizes, 7" and 5.5", #4293, sticker. These are usually found in pairs of the same size. $18-20 large, $15-18 small.

Bluebird bank, rhinestone eyes, 5.75", #267, "Geo Z Lefton," stamp. (*Courtesy of Mike & Cindy Schneider*) $55-60.

Grandma "Retirement Fund" banks, two sizes, 7" and 5.5", #4266, sticker. These are usually found in pairs of the same size. $18-20 large, $15-18 small.

Wall hanging kitchen bank, "©Geo Z. Lefton, 9.5", #087." $35-40.

Pink puppy bank with felt ears and tail, gold ribbon bow tie, rhinestone eyes , 6", #3872, sticker. $20-25.

Little girl bank, porcelain, 6", sticker. $20-22.

"Pin Money" purse bank with applied flowers, 4" high, #5861, sticker. $45-50.

White porcelain piggy banks with green shamrocks and "God Loves the Irish" on the side of the large one, 5.5" x 4" large, 3" x 2.5 small, stamps, stickers. (*Courtesy of Jessica Lynn Tyson*) Large $35-40, small $20-25.

Bells

Lefton bells, produced in many shapes and sizes, with applied and hand-painted florals, butterflies, and figurines, add beauty to any collection of bells.

Pink flower bell with pale green leaves and a butterfly on top, 3.5", #0113. $12-15.

Pink bell with gold trim, applied flowers, and green leaves, 3", #1041. $22-25.

Marks on #1041. Stamp used 1950-1970.

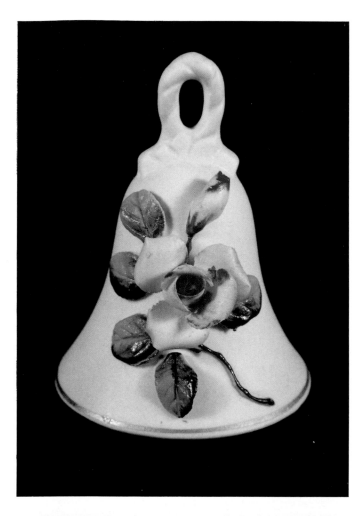

White bell with gold trim, applied flowers and leaves, 3", #1041. $18-22.

Gold trim and roses on white bell, 4.5", #428, sticker. $12-15.

White bell with gold trim and applied lilac flowers, 4", stamp, sticker. $20-25.

Floral brown Heritage bell, 3.5", #5202, stamp. $12-15

Angel Bells, August and January, two sizes, 3" and 2.5", #03257, stamp. $8-10/large, $6-8/small.

Angel Bells, October and September, two sizes, 3" and 2.5", #03257, stamp. $8-10/large, $6-8/small.

Pink porcelain bell, gold trim, 3", beautifully detailed rose, stamp. $25-30.

Brown Heritage floral bell, 5.25", #1640, sticker. $18-22.

White wedding bell with gold trim and applied pink flowers, 2", "©Geo Z Lefton." $18-23.

Green Heritage floral bell, 3.5", #5202, stamp. $12-15.

Two different anniversary bells, silver trim, 5.5" and 3", #7685, stickers. $20-23 each.

Birds

Beautiful birds have been created by the Lefton China Company, with excellent color and detail. They range from tiny to very large. There must be many bird collectors out there as I've noticed over the past year that these figurines are getting more difficult to find. With their delicate beaks and thin legs it's amazing how many there are to be found in perfect condition.

Cardinal with his head down, 4", #KW464B, stamp. $22-26.

Cardinal with his head up, 4", #KW464A, stamp. $22-26.

Two cardinals on tree limb, #2203, stamp, sticker, 4.5". $28-32.

Marks on Cardinal #KW464A. Stamp used 1955-present.

40

Mother and baby cardinal having a conversation, 5", sticker. $20-24.

Robin in bisque, #KW395, stamp, sticker, 5". $30-35.

Robin on a branch with applied flower, #00749, 2.5". $20-24.

Baby cardinal, #KW1637, stamp, sticker, 3.5". $18-20.

Robin in bisque, #KW1282, stamp, 7". $35-40.

Owl with applied flowers and leaves, #5763, sticker, 8". $30-35.

Owl with yellow, orange, and brown tones. #03999, sticker, 1983, 5". $25-30.

Marks on robin #KW1282. Stamp used 1955-present.

Bisque owl, #KW121, sticker, 4.5". $20-25.

Magnificent owl, #2235, stamp, 6.5". $30-35.

Baby robin, #KW1637, stamp, sticker, 3.5". $18-20.

Baby owls with bird, squirrel, and applied flowers, #9446, sticker, 3.25". $10-12 each.

This owl is one of the Nest Egg Collection, 5", #06874. $45-50.

Marks on #06874. Stamp used 1955-present; Taiwan sticker.

Tag that comes with the Nest Egg Collection pieces.

Nest Egg Collection hawk, 1988, #06707, "© Geo Z Lefton," stamp, sticker, 5". $50-55.

Nest Egg Collection cardinal, 4", #00244. $30-35.

Mom feeding two babies, "Waxwing" on front, 5", #KW3505. $50-55.

Marks on #00244.

Marks on waxwing #KW3505. Stamp used 1955-present.

Yellow porcelain parakeets with applied pansies, sticker, 5". $30-35.

Nest Egg Collection cardinal, 6", #00401. $40-45.

Marks on #00401.

Green and blue parakeets, (beautiful detail), #KW467, stamp, sticker, 6". $55-60.

Bluejay, 7.5", #KW395. $30-35.

Bluejay, #00749, 2.5". $18-22.

Marks on #KW395.

Pair of bluejays, 4.25", stamp, sticker. $25-30.

Goldfinch, #01886, stamp, sticker, 4". $25-30.

Baby goldfinch, #03305, 3". $18-20.

Pair of goldfinches, #00130, sticker, 3". $20-25.

Pair of pheasants, #KW769RA and #KW769LB, stamps, 5.5". $100-115 pair.

Pair of ducks, #KW618, stamp, 5". $90-100 pair.

Canary, #KW1251, 4". $16-20.

Quail, male and female, 6" and 4.5", #KW760A and #KW760B. $95-110 pair.

Pelican, #04006, copyright 1983, "Geo Z Lefton," stamp, 3". $20-25.

Marks on quail #KW760A. Sticker used 1960-1983, stamp used 1955-present.

Heron, #KW1532, stamp, sticker, 5". $55-60.

Peacock with applied flowers, #KW2336, stamp, 6". $35-40.

White dove, #KW4037, stamp, 6". $45-50.

Marks on peacock #KW2336. Stamp used 1955-present.

Pink flamingo with baby, 8". $75-80.

Mark on flamingo. Stamp used 1948-1953.

Road runner, 7", #KW3209, sticker. $75-80.

Pair of porcelain roosters, 8" and 6", large red stickers. (*Courtesy of Carol and Chuck Hanna*) $50-55 for pair.

Rooster and hen, 9" and 7", #2396, stickers. $40-45.

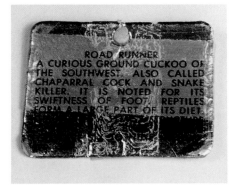

Tag describing Road Runner, #KW3209.

Pair of porcelain roosters, stickers, 4" and 6". $35-40.

Pair of ducklings, stickers, 4". $10-12 each.

Duckling with egg, #644, stamp, 3". $8-10.

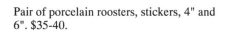

Baby chick, #01008, sticker, 2.75". $8-10.

Baby chicks, stickers, 4". $8-10 each.

Duckling with egg, #01355, stamp, sticker, 3". $8-10.

Christmas

A large variety of Lefton Christmas items are on the secondary market today. Used only once a year and for a very short time, most of the Christmas pieces can be found in excellent condition, even the oldest ones. The choices are usually priced reasonably at flea markets, second-hand stores, and antique malls. The green-and-white Holly series is highly sought after, as are the angel figurines.

Elfette in green suit with red hair, 4", sticker. $25-30.

Elfette in green suit with red hair, 4", sticker. $25-30.

Candle holder, red boot with little angel boy on top, 5", #1906, sticker. $28-32.

Holly and gold buckle on red boot, 4.5",
#2306, sticker. $25-30.

Nut and candy dish or wall hanging (has
small holes on back for string or wire), little
girl in red coat, 6.75", #443P, stamp, sticker.
$18-22.

Vase, little girl with red coat carrying holly,
6.5", #438P, stamp, sticker. $15-18.

Marks on dish #443P. Stamp was used 1955-
present. Sticker was used 1955-present,
stamp 1960-1983.

Elf candle holders, adorable little guys in red
suits and hats, 3.5", stamps. $15-18 each.

Sled planter with little girl, presents, and candy cane rutters, 5" high, "©Geo Z Lefton," large red sticker, 1956. $35-40.

Double-sided mug. Winking Santa face with candy cane handle, 3.5", #YU868. $25-30.

Cute Santa mug, 3", sticker. $10-12.

Elf head planter with large green eyes and santa hat, 5". $25-30.

The other side of the Winking Santa face, Mrs. Claus wearing glasses.

Hand-painted Christmas tree mug, white with red trim, #2834, sticker. $12-15.

Marks on elf head planter. Unusual stamp, large red sticker.

Marks on double sided mug #YU868. Stamp used 1950 to at least 1970.

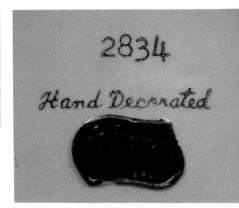

Marks on Christmas tree mug, #2834. Stamp used 1953-1971.

Kissing Santa and Mrs. Claus bisque figurines, 3", #05014, stickers. $18-22 pair.

Santa and Mrs. Claus hugging salt and peppers, 3.5", sticker. $18-22.

Mrs. Claus kissing Santa salt and peppers, 3.25". $10-15.

Three little stocking peekers, figurines with painted details, 2.5" and 3.5", stickers (# is unreadable). $15-18 each.

Marks on Santa and Mrs. Claus, 1984.

3.25" Christmas Bells, #1146, sticker. $10-15 each.

Two little 4" Christmas Bells, #1146, sticker.
$10-15 each.

White porcelain Christmas wall plate, hand painted, 8.5", #8102, stamp, sticker. $25-30.

Figurine, little girl in a red dress and white trim, pretty eyes, 3.5", #08283, stamp. $15-18.

Marks on plate #8102. Stamp used 1955-present.

Little angel figurincs with harp, violin, and music book, applied trim on bottom of robes, 4.25", #S286, A, B, and C, stickers. $35-40 each.

Christmas wall plate, hand painted on white porclain, 8.5", #450, stamp, sticker. $25-30.

Three little boy figurines with song book, violin, and light, hand painted, 5", #072. $30-35 each.

White bisque poinsetta ash tray, 6", #KW223, stamp. $18-22.

Marks on #KW223. Different stamp.

Marks on boy figurine #072. Stamp used 1950 to at least 1970. Sticker used 1953-1971.

KW 223
ASH TRAY
NOT FOR TABLE WARE

White cup and saucer with holly berries and gold trim. #2320. $25-30.

Marks on saucer #2320. Stamp used 1949-1964. Sticker used 1953-1971.

Little girl figurine singing carols, 4.5", "©Geo Z Lefton," large red sticker. $30-35.

2320

2300
DECEMBER
HOLLY

Marks on cup #2320. Stamp used 1949-1964.

Pair of white holly candle holders, 4.5"
across base, #2029, sticker. $28-33 pair.

White holly candy dish, 7" long, #6056,
1970/71, sticker. $18-22.

Bisque angel figurine playing the flute,
white with gold hair, wing tips, and holly
berries, 4", #01301, sticker, stamp. $10-12.

Little Miss Mistletoe figurine tying her
slipper, 4", #107, "©Geo Z Lefton." $35-40.

Candy cane kid, 4", "©Geo Z Lefton,"
sticker. $10-12.

Angel bell playing violin, white with gold
trim, 3.5", #1418, sticker. $18-22.

Santa Christmas mug, 4", #7235, sticker. $12-15.

Little porcelain angel figurine playing the flute, 4", #6394, sticker. $12-15.

Pitcher and bowl set with Christmas tree, 3.5" pitcher, 4.5" across bowl, #1074, stamp, sticker. $20-25.

Little girl and boy candle holders with green holly around heads, gold trim on wings and bottom of robe, 4", #5918, black sticker. $30-35 pair.

Marks on boy candle holder #5918. Black sticker possibly used 1960-1983.

White holly candle holder, 5", sticker, stamp, 1976/77. $20-25 pair.

Snowman and friend salt and pepper, 3",
#04164, stamp. $8-10 pair.

Little girl bell with song book, 4", #6604,
sticker. $30-35.

Little deer salt and pepper shakers, white
with gold antlers and hoofs, 3", #1669,
stickers. $12-15 pair.

Little girl planter with hat and muff in red,
green, and gold trim, "©Geo Z. Lefton,"
1957, 5", #166, large red sticker.
$20-25.

Two Christmas puppies with red hats and
green collars, 4" and 3", #XH7069, stickers.
$ 10-12 each.

Marks on Christmas puppies #XH7069.
Stickers used 1962-1990.

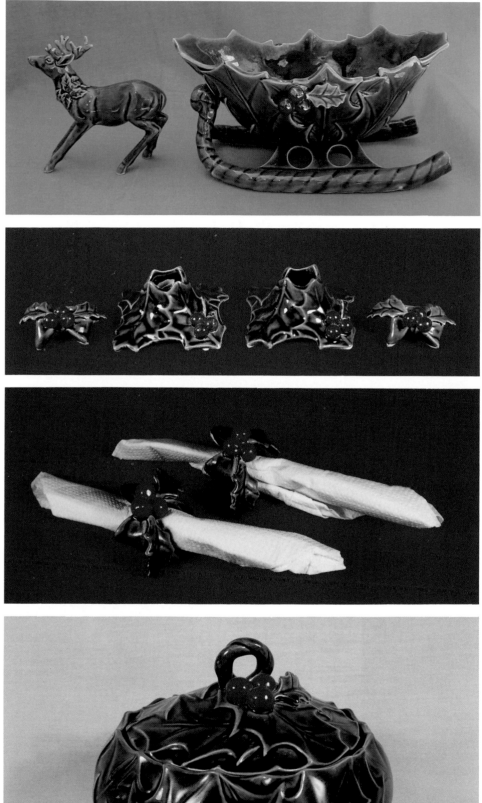

Large 8" x 4" Green Holly sleigh dish, #1346, sticker. $55-65. Green Holly reindeer figurine, 4", #1187. $18-22.

Green Holly candle holders with candle climbers, 3" holders, #1360, sticker. $25-30 for pair of holders.

Green Holly candle climbers being used as napkin rings. $10-12 each.

Covered candy dish, Green Holly, 5.5", #1361, sticker. $28-32.

Green Holly creamer and sugar, 3", #1355N, sticker. $45-50 pair.

Pair of leaf-shaped Green Holly mint dishes, 7.5" long, #1347, stickers. $25-30 each.

Candle Holders, Green Holly, 2", #6027. $28-32 pair.

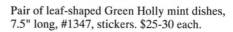

Salt and pepper shakers, Green Holly, 3", #1353. $20-25.

Little miss Green Holly bell, 4.5", #3750, sticker. $20-25.

Marks on candle holders #6027. Black sticker possibly used 1960-1983.

Bell-shaped Green Holly platter, 12", #4859, sticker. $45-50.

Salt and pepper shakers, Green Holly boots, 3", #5179. $20-25.

One-tier Green Holly tidbit dish, 7.5" across, #1364, sticker. $40-45.

6" Green Holly teapot, #1357, sticker. $80-85.

Pair of Green Holly bells, 4", #6003, 1970, black sticker on one, red sticker on the other. $10-15 each.

Cookie Jars and Canister Sets

Cookie jar collecting has been going on for many years and Lefton offers some of the very finest! Dainty Miss, Miss Priss, and Bluebird are among the whimsical figures that are in great demand today, as are the Winking Santa, Chef Girl, and Honey Bee. Lefton canister sets are still used in many kitchens and can be found in fruit and floral designs. These don't have to be limited to a kitchen, either, as that extra canister set not only looks great but is very useful in a craft-making area to hold all the odds and ends.

Cookie jar, shy pig in orange and yellow, 9.5", sticker. $70-75.

Dainty Miss cookie jar, 7.5", #040. $175-200.

Marks on #040. Stamp used 1950-1970.

Green Orchard cookie jar, #3733, 10". $65-70.

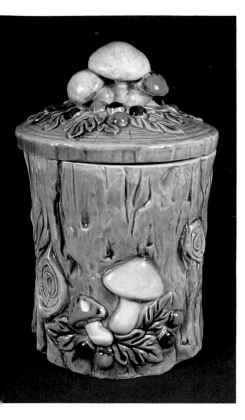

Adorable Miss Priss cookie jar, 7.5", #1502. $150-175.

Mushroom Forest cookie jar, 10.5", #6353, "© Geo Z Lefton, 1970." $50-60.

Cookie jar, chicken on nest, #1019, sticker. $75-85.

Four-piece canister set, Pear 'N Apple. Flour canister has "©Geo Z Lefton," sticker, and #4131 on bottom; sugar and coffee canisters have sticker. $115-135 set of four.

Marks on Pear 'N Apple cookie jar #4131. Sticker used 1953-1971. Stamp used 1950 to at least 1970.

Cookie jar, Pear 'N Apple, #4131, signed "©Geo Z Lefton," sticker, 10". $55-65.

Mushroom Forest canister set, four pieces, #6353. $125-145.

Two-piece canister set, gold with white and blue flowers, 7.5" and 6.5", #6447, stickers. $80-85 set of four.

Cookie jar, gold with white and blue flowers, 10", #6448, sticker. $45-50.

Covered Dishes

Whether sitting on a dresser holding jewelry or powder, on a table containing candy, nuts, or mints, or on a shelf in a china cabinet, Lefton's covered dishes are unique. They come hand painted, decorated with applied flowers and leaves, or with figurine, animal, or bird lids, in porcelain, matte, or bisque. Who knows what lurks under that lid, and who can resist peeking?

Pastel green with three feet, flowers, and gold trim, 5.5", #1084, stamp, sticker. $35-40.

Brown Heritage floral with gold trim, 5" across, #4053, stamp, $30-35.

Marks on dish #4053. Stamp used 1955-present.

Pink covered candy dish with pink and blue forget-me-not flowers and gold trim. 5", #2605, stamp, sticker. $40-45.

White candy dish with forty-two applied pink flowers and gold trim, 6", "fine hand painted china" and sticker. $65-70.

Fiftieth anniversary covered dish with three legs and gold trim, 5", #2606, stamp, sticker. $20-25.

Pink and gray with gold specks, 7" across, #8009, sticker. $35-40.

Boy sitting on lid playing instrument, applied flowers and gold trim, 3", stamp, sticker. $10-12.

White lamb with bell and applied flowers, 3.5", sticker. $12-15.

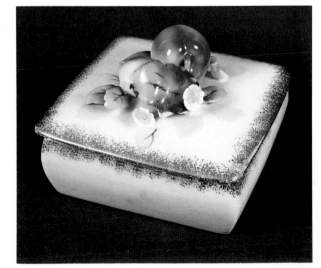

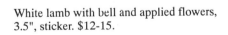

Pink covered dish, apples and flowers on lid, 4", stamp. $35-40.

Brown Heritage floral, four-footed oblong dish, 1.5", #5206. $12-15.

White dish with violets and gold trim, 4", 1961, stamp. $15-18.

Marks on white dish with violets. Stamp used 1955-present.

Red and white heart dish with two doves and applied rose and leaves on lid. 2.25", #03688, 1983. $15-18.

White porcelain heart dish, 3", "You'll never know how much it means to have a mother like you" written on the lid. #2688, sticker. $10-12.

Tiny white Hugs & Kisses heart dish with roses, 1.25", #02389, sticker. $8-10.

Cheese dish with gray mouse on top, 5.5", #H7138, sticker. $40-45.

Square white box with yellow, blue, and pink applied flowers on lid, gold trim, 2.5", sticker. $18-22.

10" x 10" four-piece tureen, Mushroom Forest, #6464. $95-110.

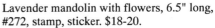

Marks on #6464. Stamp used 1950 to at least 1970.

Lavender mandolin with flowers, 6.5" long, #272, stamp, sticker. $18-20.

Round, white basket-weave porcelain dish with applied roses and leaves on lid, 2.5", sticker. $15-18.

Marks on mandolin #272. Stamp used 1955-present. Sticker used 1962-1990.

Three-footed white bisque dish with applied flowers and gold trim. 5" round, #KW3781, stamp. $35-40.

White floral covered egg dish, 5.5", #2209, stamp. $20-25.

Heart dish, white with butterflies and flowers, 4", #YA397, stamp. $22-25.

Marks on egg dish #2209. Stamp used 1946-1950.

ound dish with flowers, 3", #KW3780. *Courtesy of Irene Michul*) $15-18.

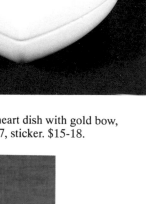

White porcelain heart dish with gold bow, 3.5" across, #1377, sticker. $15-18.

Green Heritage, round, three-footed floral pin dish with lid, 3" across, #5206, stamp. $12-15.

Green Heritage floral candy dish with gold trim, 5", stamp. $25-30.

White porcelain frog with violets, 2.25",
1958, stamp. $10-12.

Little girl powder box in yellow and white
dress with daisies, 4.5", #784, sticker. $40-
45.

Tiny, oblong, white, three-footed dish with
gold design, 2", #2310, stamp. $8-10.

Three-footed round dish with roses and gold
trim, 2", #1239, sticker. $18-20.

Marks on little girl powder box #784. Stamp
used 1953-1971.

Anniversary candy dish with bells and gold
trim, 4" high, #6508, stamp. $15-18.

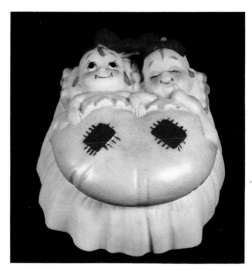

White bed box with cupie kids on lid, 3.5",
#08164, stamp, sticker. $15-18.

Anniversary sauce dish with bells and gold
trim, 4.5", #6507, stamp. $18-20.

Chick candy dish, #KW2931, 6" high. $15-18.

Instant coffee jar, 4.5", #XA397, stamp. $15-18.

Three-footed 25th anniversary candy dish, white with silver trim, 5.5" across, #998, stamp, sticker. $20-25.

Bluebird butter/cheese dish, 3.5" x 6.25", #437. $125-130.

Marks on #437. Used 1950 to at least 1970.

Cream and Sugars

Silver and gold trim. Heritage, Paisley, and Chintz. Little girls, boys, and birds. Wheat, flowers, and fruit. This is what Lefton's cream and sugars are made of.

Green Heritage floral cream and sugar, 4", #3066. $45-50.

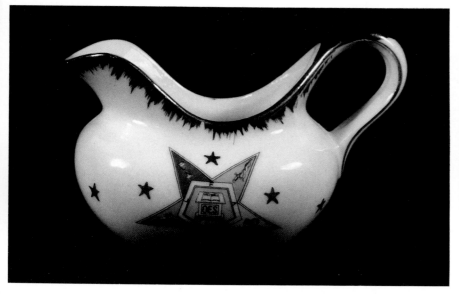

Eastern Star creamer, 2.5", #2789, stamp, sticker. $12-15.

Blue Paisley creamer, #1974, sticker, 3.5". $15-18.

Marks on creamer #2789. Stamp used 1949-1964. Sticker used 1953-1971.

Dainty Miss sugar and creamer, #322. $60-65.

Rose chintz creamer, #NE661R, sticker, stamp. $20-25.

Wheat-pattern cream and sugar, #20183. $30-35.

Miss Priss creamer, #1508, sticker. $28-32.

Sugar and creamer, Mr. Toodles, #3292, sticker. $35-40.

Small sugar and creamer, blue paisley, 2.25", #2358. $30-35.

Marks on the bottom of the blue paisley #2358. Stamp used 1946-1950.

75

Every piece that Lefton ever made is decorative and can be used to decorate a home! I have used this term for items lacking in quantity to warrant a title of their own. Lamps, musical items, bookends, and many other items fall under this category.

Sweet Violets cream and sugar (without lid), #2843. (*Courtesy of Vickie Nitecki and Irene Michul*) $25-30.

Marks on #2843. Sticker used 1953-1971.

Green Heritage floral oil lamp, 10", #4169, stamp, sticker. $85-90.

Marks on green Heritage lamp #4169. Stamp used 1955-present. Sticker used 1960-1983.

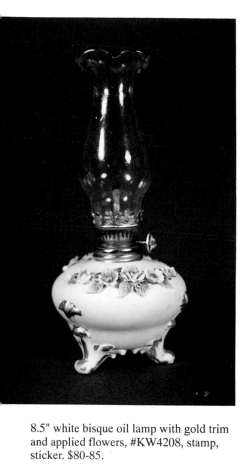

8.5" white bisque oil lamp with gold trim and applied flowers, #KW4208, stamp, sticker. $80-85.

White oil lamp with violets, 5.5", #686V, stamp. $45-50.

Night light, adorable little girl holding basket, 6", sticker. $40-45.

Marks on oil lamp #KW4208. Stamp used 1955-present. Sticker used 1960-1983.

Marks on oil lamp #686V. Stamp used 1949-1964.

Angel night light, bisque, 7", #7368. $75-80.

Boy in light blue, night light, 6.5", #6625, sticker, $40-45.

Musical valentine girl, 7", sticker, Sankyo, Japan stamped on bottom. $40-45.

Porcelain musical birthday girl, 5.5", sticker, $35-40.

Blue Boy and Pinkie musical couple, 7", #KW1107, sticker, plays "Love Story." $125-130.

Musical bluebird, sounds like the bird is chirping, 7", #7229, sticker. $45-50.

Puppy bookends, 5.5", stickers. $35-40.

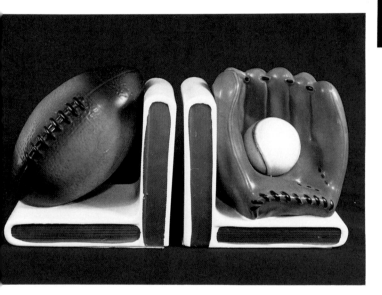

Bookends, football and baseball, 5", #H067. $35-40.

White cat bookends, 6", #H510. $38-42.

Egg cups, 3", stamp, violets, and Elegant Rose. $15-18 each.

Cheese plate with knife, 9" across, #916, sticker. $20-25.

Small basket with violets and gold trim, 3",
#03163. $10-12.

Mushroom Forest basket, 4" high, #6473,
sticker. $18-22.

Marks on #03163. Sticker used 1960-1983.
Stamp used 1955-present.

Oblong pale pink picture frame with pink
and blue flowers, gold trim, 5" X 3", #271,
stamp. (*Courtesy of my grandaughter,
Jessica Lynn Tyson*) $22-25.

White Cornucopias with pink roses, bisque,
7.5", #672, stamp. $110-120 pair.

Marks on #672. Unusual stamp.

Square pale blue picture frame with hand-painted forget-me-nots, 5", #669, stamp, sticker. (*Courtesy of my grandaughter, Nicole Marie Osborn*) $20-23.

Birdbath candle holder, white with three birds, applied flowers, and gold trim. 4", #KW499. $35-40.

Anniversary candle holder, #YA7789, sticker. $15-20.

White hobnail birdbath with applied roses, 4", #6077, stamp, sticker. $38-42.

White Candle holder birdbath with birds, gold trim, and applied pink flowers, 5.5", #087. $38-42.

Porclain shopping bag with violets and handles, 4", #2210, stamp. $20-23.

Pair of pink candle holders with roses and gold trim, 5" base, sticker. $70-75.

Shopping bag with handles and bluebird, 4",
#02385, sticker. (*Courtesy of Victoria
Colish*) $20-23.

Basket, hot poppy, 4.5", #4597. $15-20.

Pin cushion girl in yellow, white, and green,
4", #543, stamp. $15-18.

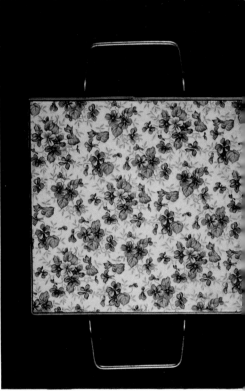

Violet chintz hotplate, sticker, 6" square.
$12-15.

Shopping bag with flowers and blue bows,
4", #2621, stamp. (*Courtesy of Victoria
Colish*) $20-23.

Green Heritage ring holder, 2.75", #5207,
stamp, sticker. $20-25.

Streetcar, sticker, "GZ Lefton licensee" on side. $30-35.

Pink bucket planter with handle, fruit, and gold trim, 3.5". $40-45.

Bottom mark on pink bucket planter.

Dishes, Tidbits, and Compotes

Lefton has produced dishes for everything! Nuts, candy, and lemon dishes. Nappys, coasters, and teabag holders. Single and double bonbons. Bone dishes, three-compartment relish dishes, egg holders, spoon rests, one-, two-, and three-high tidbits, and the most beautiful compotes painted in flowers or fruit with silver and gold trim.

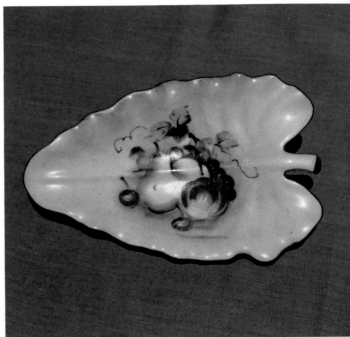

Green Heritage fruit, candy dish, 7" long, #6283, stamp. $20-25.

White Misty Rose dish with gold trim, 5", #928, stamp, sticker, "Japan" sticker. $12-15.

Marks on #928.

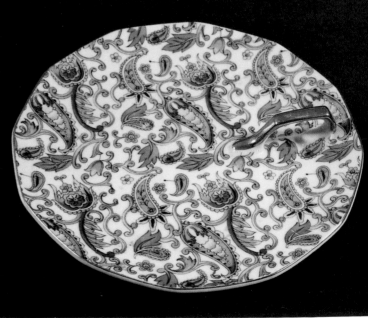

Round Blue Paisley lemon dish, 6", #NE2141, stamp. $18-22.

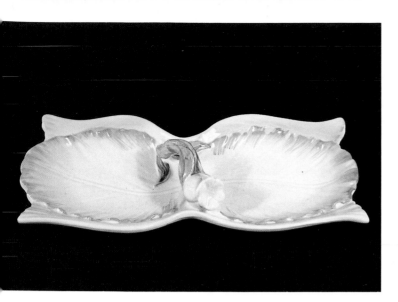

Two-compartment, yellow-and-white flowered dish, 10" long, #20313, sticker. $35-40.

Green Heritage fruit, candy dish, 6.5", #6283, stamp. $15-20.

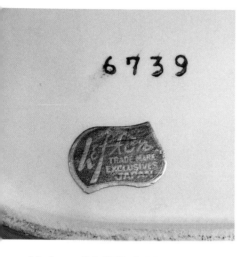

Marks on dish #20313. Sticker used 1960-1983.

25th Anniversary dish, 10" long, #1640, stamp. $25-30.

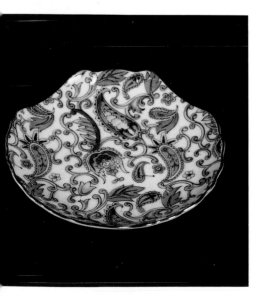

Lemon dish, Blue Paisley, 6" across, #NE2350, stamp. $18-22.

Marks on Anniversary dish #1640. Stamp used 1955-present.

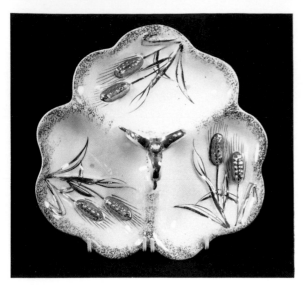

Three-compartment, wheat pattern, 9",
#20313, large red sticker. $40-45.

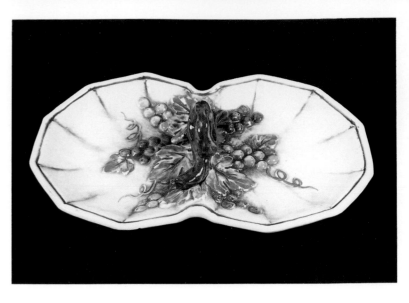

Two-compartment dish with purple and blue
berries, 8", #3034, sticker. $35-40.

Heart dish with silver trim, 5", #5971, "bone
china," signed "©Geo Z Lefton." $18-22.

Three-compartment dish, Eastern Star, 5"
long, sticker. $20-25.

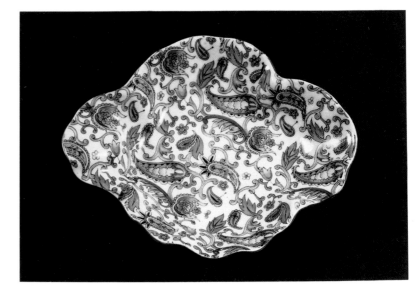

Blue Paisley candy dish, 6.5", #NE2349,
stamp. $20-22.

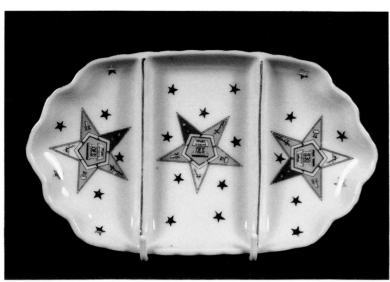

White hobnail milk glass with gold trim, 4"
across, stamp, sticker. $15-18.

Gold Heritage floral without lid, three footed, 4.5", #1870, stamp. $15-18.

Green Heritage floral mint dish, 6.25", #1860, stamp. $18-20.

Set of four tiny nut dishes, 3" each, #7161, stickers. $20-25.

Marks on floral mint dish #1860. Stamp used 1955-present.

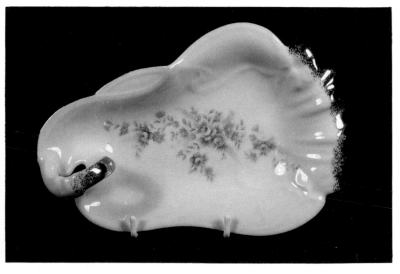

Heirloom Rose dish, 7", #7052, stamp. $28-32.

Marks on pink dish with apples.

Pink porcelain dish with apples and gold trim, 6", 1956. $25-30.

Brown Heritage floral sauce boat with underplate, 4" by 6", #5649, stamp, sticker. $85-90.

Rustic Daisy two-compartment dish, 13" long, #MR25143. (*Courtesy of Betsy Schnetzer*) $30-35.

Violet teabag holder, white with gold trim, #8262, sticker. $12-15.

Rose chintz tea bag holder with gold trim, #1793, sticker. $12-15.

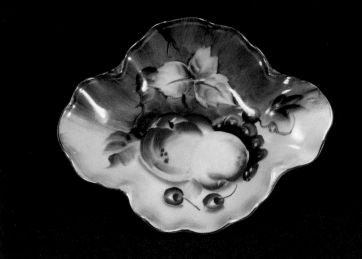

Floral candy dish in dark blues and pastel greens, 7", #NE20127B, stamp, sticker. (*Courtesy of Vicki Netecki*) $30-35.

Green Heritage tidbit, 5" high, #1153. $40-45.

Green Heritage floral two-tier tidbit, 10"
high, #1153. $85-90.

Two-tier tidbit, wheat pattern, 11" high,
#20126. $30-35.

Blue Paisley tidbit, 5" high, #NE1975,
stamp. $35-40.

Milk white compote with fruit and gold trim,
7" across, sticker, stamp. $30-35.

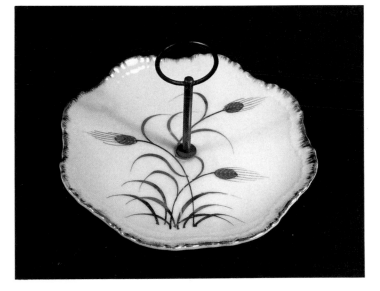

One-tier tidbit, wheat pattern, 5" high,
#20231. $25-28.

Marks on tidbit #20231. Stamp used 1946-
1953.

Rose chintz one-tier tidbit, 5" high, #NE651R-N, stamp. $35-40.

Milk white compote with roses and silver trim, 7", #NE712, stamp, sticker. (Note differences between this one and the other #NE712.) (*Courtesy of Vicki Nitecki*) $30-35.

Milk white compote with roses and silver trim, 7", #NE712, stamp, sticker. (*Courtesy of Vicki Nitecki*) $30-35.

Figurines

Boys, flower girls, bloomer girls, men, women, couples, and whimsical figures, in periods dating from Provincial to Gay Nineties, story book era to modern, from faraway China to the realms of Kewpies and Cupids—Lefton China produces all of these. A collector of figurines can be proud to add any of these to their collections.

Girls

Girl with bunny, #8613, sticker. $35-40.

This beauty is a Lefton doll house original, complete with orginal tag, 7", #6987, sticker. $50-60.

Girl powdering her nose, 4", #903, sticker. $28-32.

Girl feeding bird, 5", #KW1700B, matte, stamp. $40-45.

Girl holding a pink rose, 6.5", #KW340B, stamp, sticker. $30-35.

Girl at mailbox, 5", #KW1700, matte. $40-45.

Little 4" girl, #KW6528, stamp. $25-30.

Girl with flower, 4.5", #KW2817A, stamp, sticker. $30-35.

Girl with flower, 4.5", #KW2817, stamp. $30-35.

Birthday girl series #549-6, 3", stamp. $18-22.

Porcelain girl with flowers, 4.5", #2643, sticker. $30-35.

Little girl with basket and umbrella, 4.5", #KW334B. $30-35.

Girl holding puppy, 4.5", #KW6718. $30-35.

Marks on #KW334B.

Little girl with basket, painted flowers on dress, 4.5", #KW5154, stamp, sticker. $38-40.

Girl with flowers and basket, 4", porcelain, #1450B, sticker. $28-32.

Girl leading a duck with a ribbon, 4.5", #KW1553. $30-35.

Little girl, looks as if she's having a conversation with the duck, 4", #02891, stamp. $28-32.

Matte girl holding two flower baskets, 6", #2340B, stamp. $38-42.

Girl graduate, 4.5", stamp, #01798, sticker. $22-28.

Barefoot girl holding up dress, 4", sticker, stamp. $22-28.

Plain Taiwan sticker with no other marks on girl holding up dress.

Pretty little miss, 3.5", "care for me and keep me near" on bottom, #00329, stamp, sticker. $25-30.

Girl with two baskets of flowers, 4.5",
#KW118A, matte, stamp. $40-45.

Little graduate, 4.5", porcelain, #04415,
stamp. $22-28.

Girl sewing, 3.75", #AH901, sticker and
"Little Seamstress" on bottom of piece. $35-
40.

Little girl playing croquet, matte, 6",
#KW8006, stamp. $28-32.

Girl washing clothes. 5.5", #AH1H and
"Monday Wash" on piece. $35-40.

Little girl feeding baby, 5.5", #1110, sticker and "Feeding Time" on bottom of piece. $35-40.

Girl with bunny, bottle, and dog, 5.5". #AH1D. $35-40.

Marks on #1110. Sticker used 1953-1971.

Marks on #AH1D. Sticker used 1962-1990.

Girl with walking stick and kitten, 4.5", #TWDO2539. $35-40.

Marks on #TWDO2539. Stamp used 1955-present.

Girl with pink applied rose in hair, 4.5" #KW843B, stamp. $38-42.

Little Bo Peep story doll, 4", #1052, stamp, sticker. $50-55.

Nurse with blue dress and white apron, 4.5", #2902, sticker. $30-35.

Marks on Little Bo Peep. Stamp used 1946-1950. Sticker used 1946-1953.

Lady with basket of flowers and blue flowers painted on dress, 6", #398B, sticker. $55-60.

Lady with multi colored dress, 5.5", #2347A. $40-45.

Lady with basket of flowers, matte, 6.25", #KW335A, stamp, sticker. $50-55.

Lady, 7", #4232. $60-65.

Lady with parasol, 5.75", #KW1569. $85-90.

Colonial lady with bonnet and muff, gold trim, 5.75", #KW10566B, large red sticker, stamp. $85-90.

Marks on #4232.

Marks on #KW1569. Sticker used 1946-1953. Red stamp used 1946-1950. Black stamp used 1950 to at least 1970. Unusual with two different stamps on the same piece, plus a sticker.

"Marilyn" pose, 6", #411, sticker. $90-95.

Lady wearing large hat and holding purse, bisque, 6", #KW1703A, sticker. $65-70.

Lady wearing large hat and shawl, bisque, 6", #KW1703B, sticker. $65-70.

Tiny 4" lady with blue-and-white dress and hat, painted-on blue flowers, applied flowers in hand, sticker. $28-32.

Series #3080, 4", matte, Bloomer Girl holding skirt up in front, pastel green and brown tones. $40-45.

Beautiful face on this little lady, flair skirt, 6", matte, sticker. $45-50.

Lady with hat, parasol, purse, and lacy gold trim, 6.5", #KW10566. Piece has two different stamps: "©Geo Z Lefton" used 1950 to at least 1970, and "Lefton China, crown, Hand painted, Reg. US Pat. Off.," used 1949-1964. (*Courtesy of Linda Stutzman*) $85-90.

Series #3080, 4", matte, Bloomer Girl in pastel green and brown tones. $40-45.

This is the back of Bloomer Girl, #3080.

Two little porcelain Bloomer Girls, 4",
#1412 and #1702. $55-60 each.

Poor Bloomer Girl, scared by a mouse and
lost her bloomers! 5.25", matte, #KW1234.
$45-50.

Marks on #1412. Stamp used 1950-1957.
Sticker used 1953-1971.

Marks on #KW1234. Sticker used 1953-
1971. Stamp used 1955-present.

Marks on original box for Bloomer girl
#1702.

Series #576, Bloomer Girl, 3.5", porcelain.
$55-60.

Porcelain, 4" Bloomer Girl, stamped "©Geo
Z Lefton," series #1698. (*Courtesy of Linda
Stutzman*) $55-60.

Bloomer-type girl in yellow dress, shoes,
and bow, 4", #H4038, sticker. $35-40.

She's a 4" Bloomer Girl holding a present,
matte, #KW2322, sticker. $55-60.

Porcelain, 4" Bloomer Girl, series #1698.
(*Courtesy of Linda Stutzman*) $55-60.

Marks on #1698. Stamp used 1950 to at
least 1970.

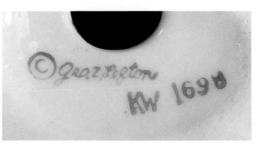

Bloomer girl with dog and umbrella, 5.5",
#6584B, stamp, sticker. $55-60.

102

Boys

Series #2300, 4.75", January boy holding the clock on his side. $30-35.

Series #2300, 5.25", January boy holding a clock on his knee. $30-35.

Series #2300, 3.75", April boy holding umbrella, sticker. $30-35.

Series #2300, 5.25", November boy with turkey, sticker. $30-35.

Ouch! Bowling boy, 4.5". $28-30.

Boy playing banjo to rabbit, 5", #8805, sticker. $20-25.

Series #2300, 5", December boy putting on Santa suit, sticker. $30-35.

Marks on bowling boy. Top stamp used 1949-1964. Bottom stamp used 1950 to at least 1970. Sticker used 1953-1971.

Barefoot boy with a fishing pole, apple, and dog. 4", #2722, sticker. $35-40.

Tom Sawyer-type boy, barefoot, 5.5", #KW845, bisque. $60-65.

Accordion boy, 5", bisque, #KW5827. $28-32.

Train boy, 5", signed "©Geo Z Lefton," #4648. $35-40.

Marks on boy #KW845. Stamp used 1955-present.

March boy flying a kite, 4", #6343, sticker. $20-25.

Little fisherman with broken pole, 5", #1240, sticker. $50-55.

Boy graduate, 5", #2791, sticker. $30-35.

Boy with sheet music, 5.5", #SH1A, sticker and "The Singer" on bottom of piece. $35-40.

Boy with newspapers, 6", #AH1B and "Newsboy" on bottom of piece. $35-40.

Boy graduate, 5", #2791, (note differences between this one and the other #2791), sticker. $30-35.

Little Irish boy, 4", #KW4461. $18-22.

This little guy is from the Heavenly Hobo series, 4", #04630, stamp. $40-45.

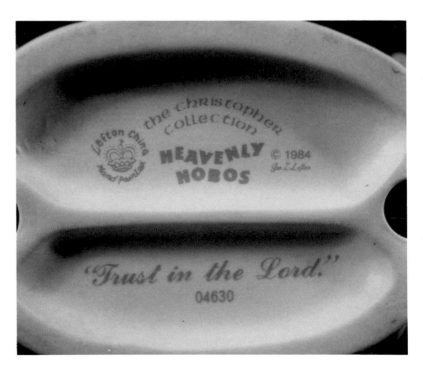

Marks on #04630.

Miscellaneous Figurines

Sad bisque Kewpie, 3", #KW228. $30-35.

Kewpie baby with big eyes, 3.5", #4132, sticker. $28-30.

Kewpie #2175, stamp, sticker. $30-35.

...tor with newborn, 8", #G5747, stamp,
...ker. $35-40.

Man with a camera, 8", #XIL303A, stamp,
sticker. $35-40.

Bust of Chopin, 5.5", #KW1166. $25-30.

Marks on Chopin #KW1166. Stamp used
1955-present.

Marks on #G5747. Stamp used 1953-1975,
sticker used 1962-1990.

Football guy, 7.5", #2777, stamp, sticker.
(*Courtesy of Denise Mannino*) $35-40.

Mozart bust, 5.5", #KW1180. $25-30.

Green elf asleep on a log, 3.5", #3522, "©Lefton." $20-25.

Three little Leprechauns, 4", #6203, stickers. $23-28 each.

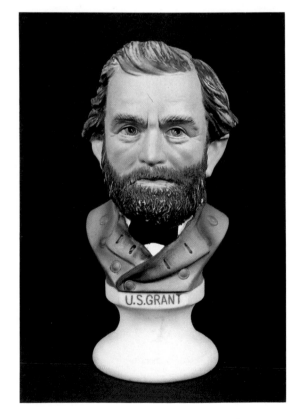

Bust of U. S. Grant, 5.5", #KW2297. $25-30.

Marks on Leprechaun with trumpet. Stamp used 1960-1983.

Two Irish gents dancing and playing a fiddle, 4", stickers. $23-28 each.

Chinese boy and girl shelf sitters with applied rhinestones, 4", #KW127, sticker. $50-55 pair.

Oriental couple with applied rhinestones, 5.5". $75-80 pair.

Children in a kissing booth, 4.75", #07821, sticker. $20-25.

Marks on Oriental couple. Stamp used 1950-1957. Sticker used 1946-1953.

School children, 5", #SH1G, sticker and "Tutoring" on bottom of piece. $35-40.

Provincial couple with jugs, 7.5",
#KW5641, stamp, sticker. $200-225.

Bride and groom, 4.5", #4703, sticker. $20-25.

Blue Boy and Pinkie Victorian couple, 8",
bisque, #KW387. $300-325 pair.

Colonial children on love seat, matte, 4.5"
high, #4903, sticker, stamp. $55-60.

Cupie couple, 2.5" and 3", #03268, sticker.
$25-30.

Marks on Blue Boy. Sticker used 1962-1990.

Marks on Pinkie. No stamp or sticker.

Colonial man holding grapes, applied flowers, 8", #KW3047N-A, stamp. $100-110.

Bride and groom, 5.5", "©Geo Z Lefton," #06372, stamp. $28-32.

Marks on #KW3047N-A. Stamp used 1955-present.

Christopher Collection
(Little Treasures)

This tag is found on most of the Christopher Collection Series.

March boy playing soccer, 3.75". $20-25.

February boy playing hockey, 3.75". $20-25.

May boy playing golf, 3.75". $20-25.

June boy playing tennis, 3.75". $20-25.

November boy with a hunting rifle, 3.5". $20-25.

December boy on a bobsled, 3.75". $20-25.

Flower girl, January, 4.5", #03911. $20-25.

September boy playing basketball, 3.75". $20-25.

Marks on #03911.

Little girl holding basket of kittens, 5",
#03459. $20-25.

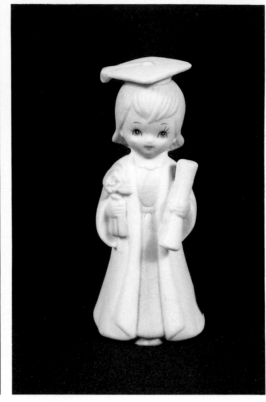

Girl graduate, 3.5", #03803. $20-25.

Bride and groom kids, 4", #03827, 1983,
sticker. $25-30.

Girl angel ringing bell, 5", #00334. $20-25.

Boy graduate, 3.5", #03805. $20-25.

Hands

The Lefton hands are beautiful! No word can describe them as well. From the tiny ashtrays, ring holders, and mint or nut dishes to the large planters and vases, the hands are so lifelike and delicate in detail and form.

Hands dish, applied roses, and gold trim, 7.5", stamp. $40-45.

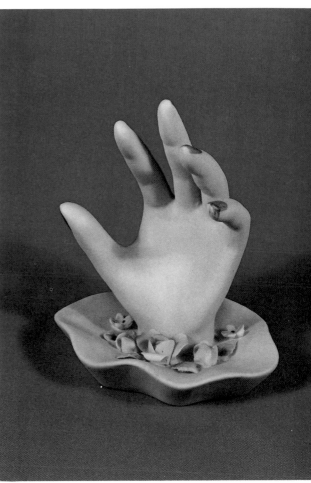

Pink hand ring holder with rose and gold-painted fingernails, bisque, 4" high, #1444, sticker. $18-22.

Hand holding pink rose, gold trim and flower on wrist, porcelain, 5" long, stamp, sticker. $35-40.

Porclain pink hands decorated with pansies and gold trim, 6" high, sticker, stamp. $45-50.

Double hands, porcelain, decorated with applied leaves and flowers, 7". $50-55.

Double hands holding a vase with applied roses and leaves, 7", #230, stamp, sticker. $65-70.

Bisque double hands decorated with flowers and gold trim, 7", KW4344, stamp, sticker. $45-50.

Mark on double hands. Stamp used 1946-1953.

Marks on hands with vase #230. Stamp used 1946-1950. Large rcd sticker used 1946-1953.

Double-hands vase, applied flowers, 7", #KW4198. $45-50.

Double hands with delicate pink flowers and gold trim, 5", #1787, stamp. $38-42.

Marks on #KW4198. Sticker was used from 1960-1983.

Heavenly Bodies (Angels)

Any angel collector will find that the very best were made by Lefton. The fine detail on most of these is extraordinary, from the tip of the wings to the bottom of the feet. There are angels for days of the week, months of the year, zodiac signs, birthdays, and holidays. Boys, girls, Kewpies, flower girls, kissing angels, climbing angels, and angels enclosed in frames are available. What a large and wonderful selection to choose from!

All three of these are March angels, 4". The first two have #KW3332 and the red sticker. The third has #3332 and the red sticker. Matte. Notice the difference in the coloring and detail. Each one is different. $28-32 each.

Angel of the Month series #3332, sticker, 4", January, matte. $30-35.

May and June angels, 4", #3332 and red sticker, matte. $28-32 each.

Both of these angels are September, 4", matte. The first has #3332 and red sticker. The second has #KW3332 and red sticker. Note the difference between the two! $28-32.

The two of these are December angels, matte, 4", #3332 and red stickers but note the differences. One is looking straight ahead and the flowers have small petals. The other is looking to the right and has larger petals. $28-32 each.

November angel, 4", #3332 and red sticker, matte. $28-32.

Angel of the Month series 4", #489. This series was made in porclain. $30-35.

July angel, 4", "Water Lily Ruby," #489, sticker and "©Geo. Z. Lefton" are on the bottom. $30-35.

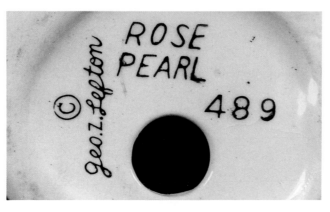

Marks on #489 angel. Stamp used 1950 to at least 1970.

August angel #489, 4". "Poppy Peridot," sticker, and "©Geo. Z. Lefton" on bottom of piece. $30-35.

November angel #489, 4", "Mums Topaz," sticker, and "©Geo. Z. Lefton" on bottom of piece. $30-35.

May angel, #6224, 4.5". $25-30.

Marks on #6224. Sticker used 1960-1980.

October angel #489, 4", "Cosmos Rosezirgon," sticker, and "©Geo. Z. Lefton" on bottom of piece. $30-35.

Angel of the Month series #6224, January, 4.5", sticker. This series was done in porcelain and a birthstone added in the center of each flower on the skirt. $25-30.

October angel, #6224, 4.5", sticker. $25-30.

Flower Girl of the Month series #985, 5", matte. $30-35.

August angel, #985, 5". August is written in the front instead of on the bottom. $30-35.

Marks on #985. Stamp used 1950 to at least 1970.

November angel, #6224, 4.5", red sticker. $25-30.

Marks on #985. Stamp used 1950-at least 1970. Sticker used 1953-1971.

Saturday's Child, 4", porcelain, # K8281, stamp. Heavier in weight than the Friday's Child. $33-38.

Sunday angel in frame, 4", porcelain, #AR6883W, 1955. This is one of a series. $30-35.

Friday's Child, 4", porcelain, #KW574, stamp. $33-38.

Marks on #AR6883W. Stamp used 1950 to at least 1970. Sticker used 1946-1953.

Two angel flower girls, yellow and blue dresses, 5", #110. $15-20 each.

January angel, 4.5", porcelain, series #1987S, "©Geo. Z. Lefton." $30-35.

August angel, 4.5", porcelain, series #1987S, "©Geo. Z. Lefton." $30-35.

June bride angel, porcelain, 3.75", #808B, 1950-1955. $33-38.

Boy and girl angels kissing on a bench, 4", porcelain, #1223, sticker. $35-40 pair.

Marks on June bride. Stamp used 1946-1950. Sticker used 1946-1953.

May angel, boy, "To Mama," 4.5, bisque, #1952, sticker. $30-35.

March angel, 3.5", #04883, stamp, "© 1985 Geo. Z. Lefton." $20-25.

Little girl angel, bisque, blue dress, playing a triangle, 4.5", #KW23796, "Japan." $20-25.

Angel bride, 4", #KW8273, stamp. $33-38.

Kissing angels, white bisque, 3.5", #02079. $15-20 pair.

Pitchers and Bowls

Pitcher and bowl collectors will find that Lefton makes some of the most beautiful ones. There are small sets with applied flowers and leaves and large sets with painted floral and fruit designs in porcelain and bisque. Large milk pitchers go with sets such as Rustic Daisy, Mushroom Forest, Dutch Girl, Pear and Apple, and the Heritage series. The variety seems endless.

Pitcher and bowl with fruit, gold trim, #6281, stamp, sticker, 3.75". $20-25.

Gold milk pitcher, #4553, 6.5". $18-22.

Pitcher and bowl with green clovers, 3.25", #03084. $20-25.

Marks on #03084. Stamp used 1955-present. Sticker used 1962-1990.

Pitcher and bowl with pink flowers and gold trim, 3.5", #4672, stamp, sticker. (*Courtesy of Debbie Roswell*) $25-30.

White pitcher with cherubs, 3.25", #3570, sticker. $18-22.

Large milk pitcher, Pear 'N Apple, 9", #4334, stamp. $25-30.

Marks on pitcher and bowl #4672. Stamp used 1955-present. Sticker used 1960-1983.

Marks on #4334. Stamp used 1950 to at least 1970.

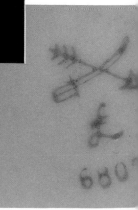

Paisley Fantasia pitcher and bowl, 5.5 pitcher, 7.5" bowl, #6807. (*Courtesy of Victoria Colish*) $55-60.

Pitcher with violets and gold trim, 5.5", #325, sticker. $25-30.

Mark on #6807. Stamp used 1971-plus.

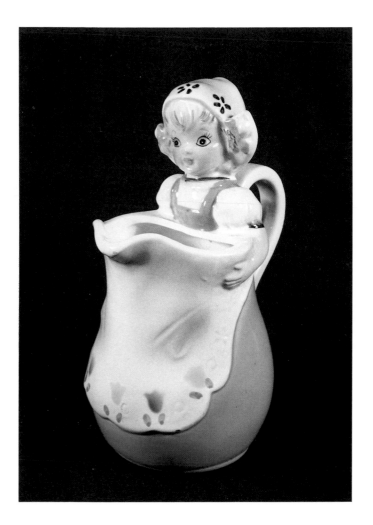

Dutch girl milk pitcher, 7", #2124, sticker, ESD hand painted, Japan. $50-55.

Anniversary pitcher and bowl, silver trim, 3.5" high, #6548, stamp, sticker. $18-22.

Planters

Lefton planters come in all sizes, shapes, and colors. There are planters for children made in animal form. Bird and people planters, planters for holidays and holy days, and gorgeous planters with applied flowers and leaves. I have found that the smallest planters work well with miniature roses, ivy, and ferns while the larger leaf vines and bulb flowers look great in the large planters. There are several books on the market today about figural planters, with some of Lefton's finest included.

Animals and Birds

Kitten planter with pink bow and roses, 4", sticker. $20-25.

Elephant planter, pink and blue marks, 6", #075, sticker. $20-25.

Planter, three Siamese kittens, 4.5", #7200, stamp. $22-25.

Siamese kitten planter with large blue eyes, 5", #H6974, sticker. $25-30.

Tiger planter with cute face, similar to the tiger bank, 6", #6818. $15-18.

White poodle planter, 7", #780. $25-30.

Swan planter, 4.5" high, white porcelain with forget-me-not flowers and leaves, #2770. $30-35.

Marks on #780. Unusual stamp.

Comical kitten planter, 5.5", #H374, sticker. $18-20.

Little bull dog planter, 5.5", # H4906. $18-20.

Cat planter with stripes, 6", #H4905. $18-20.

White lamb planter with yellow daisies and pink trim, 7", #6189. $20-25.

Marks on #H4906. Stamp used 1960-1983.

Poodle pulling cart planter, 7.5" long,
#KR50065, sticker. $35-40.

Rooster planter, bisque, 4.5", #KW1466,
stamped "Rooster" on bottom. $18-20.

Planter bird with pink, black, and yellow
coloring, 6", sticker. $30-35.

Dog planter with black top hat and green
bow, 6", #H7714. $20-25.

Pink porcelain cat planter with applied
flowers and gold trim, 6", large red sticker
and "Japan" stamp.
$30-35.

Owl planter, 6" high, #H4470, sticker. $20-
25.

Kitten planter, 7", #C7116, sticker. $28-32.

Bluebird planter, 6", #288, "©GZL," stamp,
sticker. (*Courtesy of Mike and Cindy
Schneider*) $45-50.

Oriole planter, 6.25", #3622. $20-25.

Lady planter with flower basket, 8",
#1684B, sticker. $40-45.

Marks on #3622. Sticker used 1953-1971.

adies

Lady planter, brown and tan dress, 8",
#2908, sticker. $30-35.

Lady planter, dress in browns and blues with
applied flowers, 8", #2908, sticker. $30-35.

Lady planter, light green dress with white
dots, holding flowers, 7", #1855, sticker.
$38-42.

Lovely lady planter with basket of flowers, porcelain, 6", #4226A, sticker. $30-35.

Lady planter, green dress with applied white flowers, 6", #1337A, sticker. $30-35.

Planter, lady with dark multicolored dress, 6", #2348B, sticker. $25-30.

White and yellow lady planter with basket of flowers, 6", #3000C, sticker. $25-30.

Lady planter, brown dress with applied blue, flowers, 6", #1337, sticker. $30-35.

Lady planter, blue dress with white dots, holding basket of flowers, 6", #1857, sticke $30-35.

Lady planter with plant, 6.5", #423, sticke $40-45.

Lovely lady planter with parasol and hat, 8", #500A, sticker. $55-60.

Lady planter, dress in blue tones, 6", #A277, sticker. $30-35.

Planter, lady with dark green dress, light pink applied flowers, light brown hair, 6", #50482. $40-45.

Lady planter, dress in brown tones, 6", #A277, sticker. $30-35.

Lady planter with burgundy dress, white applied flowers, auburn hair. Vines in planter, 6", #50482. $40-45.

Planter, lady with light green dress, dark pink applied flowers, yellow hair, 6", #50482. $40-45.

Marks on bottoms of all three planters #50482. Sticker used 1953-1971. Stamp used 1950 to at least 1970.

Little girl planter with green dress and hat, light yellow hair, 7", #5973, sticker. $20-25.

Planter, girl with white dress, yellow hair, 7", #MR6639, sticker. $25-30.

Little girl planter with white dress and hat, pink flowers, 7", #3138, sticker. $30-35.

Little girl planter with brown dress and hat, dark yellow hair, 7' #5973, sticker. $20-25.

Girl planter with white dress and hat, yellow daisies, 6.5", #6094, sticker. $20-25.

Girl planter with white dress and hat, yellow flowers, 7", #3138, sticker. $30-35.

Little girl planter, pastel green dress, 6", #224, sticker. $25-30.

Adorable little girl planter holding hat, 6", #246, sticker. $30-35.

Colorful Dutch girl planter, 6.5", #K662, sticker. $28-32.

Planter, little girl with pink and black dress, holding basket, 6.5", #50585, "©Geo Z Lefton." $35-40.

This little guy matches the little girl, 6", #246, sticker. $30-35.

Marks on boy planter #246. Sticker used 1953-1971.

Colorful Dutch boy planter, matches the little girl, 6.5", #K662, sticker. $28-32.

Marks on Dutch boy planter #K662. Sticker used 1960-1983.

Angel with cello planter, 7", #3097, sticker. $30-35.

Whiteware planter, "Renaissance by Lefton," 9.5", sticker. $35-40.

Angel planter, 4.5", #982. $20-25.

Marks on cello planter #3097. Sticker used 1953-1971.

Marks on angel planter #982. Stamp used 1950 to at least 1970.

Whiteware planter, "Renaissance by Lefton," 8", #H3164, sticker. $30-35.

"Renaissance by Lefton," whiteware planter, 4"x5", #3565, sticker. $25-30.

White angel Halloween planter with rhinestones, 4", "©Geo Z Lefton, 1956," #165, sticker. $20-25.

Little boy and girl sitting on pink Dutch shoes, 4.5" and 5", stamp. #5260. $65-70.

Valentine cupid planter with red hearts and gold trim, 4.5", #2995, sticker. $18-23.

Planter, kissing angels on a bench, 4", #1264, sticker. $20-25.

Black planter with gold angels on sides, 5", #415N, sticker. $28-32.

Planter, rocking chair with pipe on side, 6", #1220, sticker. $20-25.

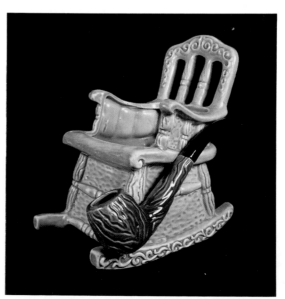

Shoe planter, white with flowers, 5"x7",
#C8507, sticker. $35-40.

White bisque planter with applied pink
flowers, gold trim, 3.75", #826, stamp,
sticker. $35-40.

Spinning wheel planter, brown, red, and
green tones, 6.5", #K7882, sticker. $18-22.

Whiteware planter with handle, ivory and
gold trim, 8.5" #194, stamp. $28-32.

Marks on planter #826. Sticker used 1953-
1971. Stamp used 1949-1964.

White hobnail planter, gold trim, 4", #8823,
stamp. $38-42.

White bisque planter, applied flowers and trim, 4", #827. $40-45.

Green porcelain planter with cherubs on sides, 6.5", #4946, sticker. $23-28.

Pink porcelain planter, applied white flowers, gold trim, 4", #553, stamp. $40-45.

Marks on planter #553. Stamp used 1949-1964.

Marks on #827. Sticker used 1953-1971. Stamp used 1949-1964.

Baseball and glove planter, 5.5", #H8085, sticker. $18-22.

Green porcelain planter, 6.5", #4550, sticker. $20-25.

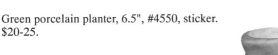

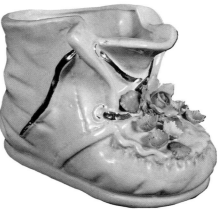

White baby shoe planter with pink trim and flowers, 4", #1811, stamp. $25-30.

Antique ivory bisque planter, egg shaped, 5.5", #722, sticker. $20-25.

Boat shaped planter, white with gold flecks, 12" long, #W1172, sticker. $28-32.

White Swan planter with applied pink roses and green leaves, 3.5", #6156, sticker. $20-25.

White flower pot with flowers and butterflies, 4", #KW1165, sticker, stamp. $15-18.

Salt and Pepper Shakers

You say you have a salt and pepper collection but have none of Lefton's? Shame on you! Reasonably priced and with a wide selection of shapes and sizes, they add so much beauty and interest to a collection. Shakers were produced to go with sets such as Miss Priss, Dainty Miss, Bluebird, Rustic Daisy, Mushroom Forest, Paisley, Chintz, and Heritage, to mention but a few.

Salt and pepper graduate owls with rhinestone eyes, 3.25". $20-25.

Graduate owl salt and peppers with rhinestone eyes, 3.5", #30145, red sticker, signed, 1956. $18-23.

Yellow salt and pepper owls with green eyes, 3", #H6836, red sticker. $10-12.

Marks on graduate owls.

White Eastern Star salt and pepper with gold trim, 3", #KF103. $8-10.

Little girl heads salt and pepper with eyes open and closed, 2.5", #1711, red sticker, black sticker reads "Made in Japan." $15-20.

Dainty Miss salt and pepper, 3", #439, sticker. $35-40.

Brown bunny salt and pepper, 2.5", #H786, stamp. $10-12.

Salt and pepper pink kittens with painted pink and blue flowers, 2.5", #1277, sticker. $18-22.

Heirloom Rose cup-shaped salt and pepper, 2.25", #6433, stamp, sticker. $15-18.

144

Miss Priss salt and pepper, 3", #1511, "Made in Japan" sticker. $35-40.

Eastern Star salt and pepper, 2.5", #3788, stamp, sticker. $8-10.

Marks on Miss Priss #1511. Sticker is oval with silver trim.

"Happy Anniversary" salt and pepper bells with gold trim and pink flowers, 3", #6293, sticker. $10-12.

Rustic Daisy salt and pepper, 7", #4142, stamp. $22-25.

White with gold trim 50th Anniversery salt and pepper, #1955, 3", $8-10.

Salt and pepper ducks, #6196, stamp, sticker. $8-10.

Marks on Rustic Daisy #4142. Stamp used 1950 to at least 1970.

Salt and pepper, gold Pear and Apple, 3.25", "©Geo Z Lefton," #3743. $10-12.

Pink Daisy salt and pepper, #5163, sticker. $8-10.

Salt and pepper pineapples with applied pink roses, 2.75", #KW3053, stamp. (*Courtesy of Sabra Cummins*) $30-35.

Saucers, Cups, and Snack Sets

Lefton produced floral and fruit, whimsical figures, tea, coffee, after-dinner cups and saucers, mustache cups, mugs, and snack sets. Many of the cups and saucers are of bone china and were produced in England. Some were signed "Geo. Z. Lefton." These are highly collectible and are becoming more difficult to find.

White pedestal cup and saucer with elegant roses and gold trim. $30-35.

Cup and saucer with roses. $25-28.

Marks on cup and saucer with roses.

Rose chintz cup and saucer, #NE656R, stamp, sticker. $18-20.

Light gray cup and saucer with flowers and gold trim, large red sticker. $25-28.

White cup and saucer with violets, stamp. $18-20.

Six Mushroom Forest mugs on stand, #6356. $15-18 each.

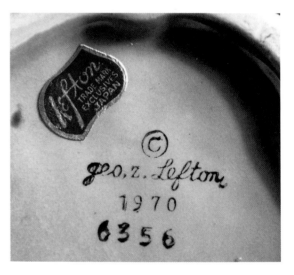

Marks on #6356 cups. Sticker used 1960-1983. Stamp used 1950 to at least 1970.

Small pedestal cup and saucer with red, gold, and black leaves, stamp, sticker. $25-28.

Eastern Star cup and saucer, #2337, stamp. $18-23.

Large Grandpa cup, #2596, sticker. $10-12.

White "Blue Jay" cup and saucer with gold trim, #E2167, stamp. $28-30.

Large Grandma cup, #2594, sticker. $10-12.

Mother mug, #434, sticker. $10-12.

White, heart-shaped saucer and three-footed cup with red and yellow roses and gold trim, stamp. $35-40.

Fruit design cup and on saucer signed Geo Z Lefton on the inside, #E2722, stamp. $50-55.

Brown Heritage fruit pattern, three-footed cup. $50-55.

Pink and gold pearlized cup and saucer, stamp. $30-35.

White cup and saucer with fruit and gold trim, stamp. $30-35.

Signature on Brown Heritage cup and saucer.

Mr. Toodles mug, #3672, sticker. $15-18.

Pearlized pastel green cup and saucer,
#NE1424, stamp. $35-40.

Violet mug-type cup with saucer, #10967,
stamp. $15-18.

Anniversary cup and saucer, stamp, sticker.
$18-20.

Western mug with gun handle, 5.5", #H171,
sticker. $35-40.

George Washington mug with feather
handle, 6", #KW2326, stamp. $38-42.

Shamrock pixie mug, 5.5", sticker. $15-18.

Marks on western mug #H171. Sticker used
1962-1990.

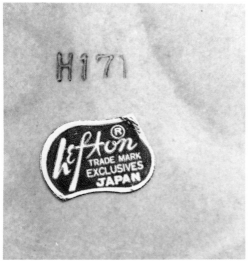

Pastel green cup and saucer with roses and gold trim, #KF801, stamp, sticker. $38-43.

Cup and saucer. Hearts, flowers, and gold trim. #1424, stamp, sticker. $35-40.

Saucer and cup, pastel blue with roses and gold trim, stamp, sticker, #KF801. $38-43.

White snack set with gold trim, sold four sets in a box, 9", #2497, stamp. $20-25 each set.

Pink pearl lustre cup and saucer, gold trim, stamp. $30-35.

Green Heritage floral snack set, sold four sets in a box, 9", #3071, stamp, sticker. $30-35 each set.

Smoking Accessories

Since smoking is fast becoming a thing of the past, related pieces are in high demand by the collector. Lefton created many smoking accessories, though it seems unlikely that these lovely pieces, with their applied flowers and leaves, were ever used for their intended purpose. Therefore most are found in perfect condition.

Pink, round ashtray with applied forget-me-not flowers, #40453, stamp, 3.5". $25-30. (*Courtesy of Lisa Osborn*)

Ashtray, black and white with a bow tie, #50564, sticker. $10-12.

Marks on ashtray #40453. Stamp used 1946-1950.

Cigarette holder and two ashtrays, Heirloom Rose, 2.5". $20-25.

Four ashtrays nested in holder, wheat pattern, sticker. $12-15.

White poodle ashtray with spaghetti fur, stamp, sticker. $28-32.

Oblong ashtray, pink with applied forget-me-not flowers, stamp. $25-30.

Round blue ashtray with applied white flowers, 3.5", #2228, sticker. $15-20.

Bowlers ashtray, 2.5" high, #H6681, sticker. $15-18. (*Courtesy of Patti Ann Neiding*)

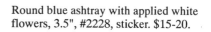

Marks on blue ashtray #2228. Sticker used 1953-1971.

White ashtray with applied pink roses and green leaves, 3.75", #1196, stamp, sticker. $20-22.

Cigarette holder with white Lily of the Valley applied flowers and green leaves, 3.5", #286, large red sticker. $35-40.

Marks on ashtray #1196. Sticker used 1953-1971. Stamp used 1949-1964.

Eastern Star ashtray, #4340, stamp. $18-22.

Small pink swan ashtray with applied pink and blue forget-me-nots, 3.5" lg., #1586, sticker. $25-30.

Spiritual

Spiritual plaques, planters, and figurines are sought after by the collectors of today. The Lefton Infant of Prague statue is a beautiful piece and comes in more than one size. The little nun planters are adorable, as are the choir girl and boy figurines. The Madonna comes in various sizes in figurines, planters, and vases, and the cherub wall hangings are lovely eye catchers.

Pink planter with the Lord's prayer, pink and blue forget-me-nots, 4". $18-22.

Two nuns with adorable expressions! 4.5" and 5.5", #K1428, stamp. $20-25 each.

Infant of Prague figurine, beautifully decorated in ceramic lace, gold, and inset stones, 4.5", #KW252S. $80-90.

Marks on nuns #K1428. Stamp used 1950 to at least 1970.

Marks on #KW252S.

Three choir boys, planter, 5", stamp, sticker,
#944. $15-20.

Planter, nun reading Bible, gold trim,
sticker, 4.5". $25-30.

White Lord's Prayer planter with pink and
yellow forget-me-nots, 4", stamp. $18-22.

Lord's Prayer planter, white with pink and
blue forget-me-nots and gold trim, 4",
stamp, sticker. $18-22.

Mary and baby Jesus planter, 10", #3646,
sticker. $30-35.

Praying nun planter, gold trim, sticker, 4.5".
$25-30.

Planter with Masonic emblem and violets, #234, sticker. $15-18.

Madonna bust, white with gold trim, 4", $25-30.

Sleeping cherub in bisque, 3", #432, comes as a pair with one awake, $85-90 for pair, or $40-45 single.

Teapots and Coffee Pots

Seldom do we see coffee and teapots being used unless it's a special occasion. To keep these coffee pots and teapots from being just more items in a china cabinet, and being the flower and plant lover that I am, I have found that they will hold both flower and plant arrangements without damage to the inside. I use double plastic sandwich bags filled with soil as inserts. Keeping the inside clean is then easy. This method can also be used for all vases and planters to keep them looking nice.

Dainty Miss teapot, #321. $145-155.

Six-cup Green Heritage teapot, #792, 8". $95-120.

Rose chintz teapot holds six cups, #911, 7". $100-125.

Rustic Daisy teapot, 8", sticker, #3855. $45-50.

Coffee Pot, *fleur-de-lis*, #KF2910N, 8". $60-65.

Violet teapot with stacked creamer and sugar, #985. $180-200.

Anniversary teapot, #NE273NP, stamp, sticker. $50-60.

Blue Paisley coffee pot, #NE1972. $85-90.

Anniversary coffee pot, #6508, stamp, sticker. $50-55.

Little elf head teapot, 6" high, #3973. $140-165.

Bottom of elf head teapot.

Vases

Lefton produces a large variety of vases! Made of glass, bisque, matte and porcelain, they come in many sizes and shapes, with applied or hand-painted flowers, leaves, and trim. There are short, fat, tall, thin, and handle vases, head vases, egg and pineapple shapes, and hand-blown glass vases, to name but a few.

White porcelain vase with flowers and gold trim, 6.25", #MM191, stamp. $20-25.

Pink porcelain vase with flowers and gold trim, 6.25", #131, stamp, sticker. $20-25.

White with painted flowers and gold trim, 7.25", #7160, stamp. $10-12.

Pair of pink porcelain vases with forget-me-not flowers, 7.5", stamp, sticker. $40-45 each.

Three-footed, egg-shaped vase with painted-on flowers, 3.5", #8189, stamp, sticker. $12-15.

White bisque with handle and applied pink and yellow flowers, 7", #459, sticker. $25-30.

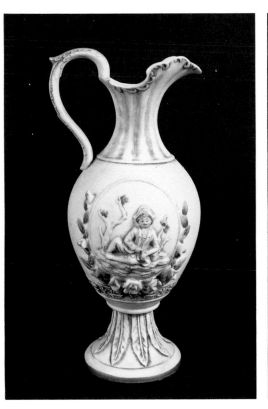

Cornucopia with rhinestones, lilacs, and gold trim. 6". #158, stamp, $55-60.

Ivory-colored vase with handle and Colonial boy, 7", #KW156, stamp, sticker. $25-30.

Pink fluted vase with forget-me-not flowers, gold trim, 4.5", stamp, sticker. $35-40.

Pink vase with pearls and rhinestones in forget-me-not flowers, gold trim, 6", stamp. $50.00-55.00.

White with basket weave around bottom, pink flowers, 6.25", #05130. $23-28.

White bisque with gold trim and applied pink roses. 6.5", #828, stamp. $40-45.

Marks on vase #05130, Taiwan sticker.

Fluted pink vase with forget-me-not flowers and gold trim, 4.5", stamp, $35-40.

White vase with pink square bottom, gold trim and pink roses. 6.5", #K7278. $35-40.

Mark on #K7278. Stamp used 1946-1950.

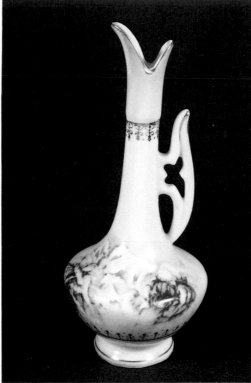

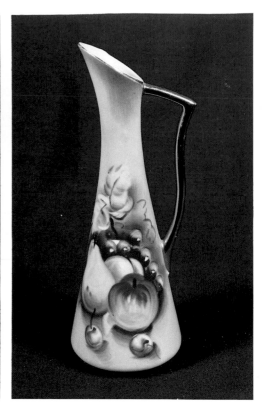

White porcelain hobnail vase with applied pink roses, fluted top, gold trim. 6.25", #830, stamp, sticker. $15-20.

Green Heritage floral with gold trim, 5.5", #5695. $20-23.

Brown Heritage fruit with handle and gold trim, 5.5", #NE2764, stamp.$18-20.

Marks on #5695. Stamp used beginning in 1968.

Exquisite white with applied flowers, handle, and gold trim. 5", #KW4196, stamp, sticker. $20-25.

White bisque with gold trim, pink roses, and handle, 7", #829, stamp. $30-35.

Marks on white vase #KW4196. Stamp used 1955-present. Sticker used 1960-1983.

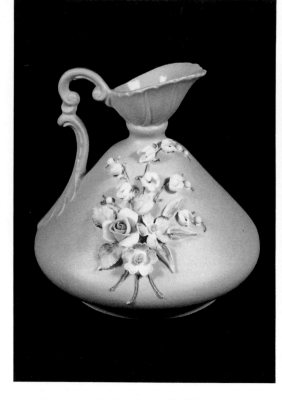

Lilac vase with handle, applied flowers, bisque, 4.5", #2940, stamp, sticker. $30-35.

Pretty lady head vase, 6.5", "Lefton's, Japan, GZL" on bottom. $85-90.

Lady head vase with pearl necklace and rhinestone earrings, 6", #2358, sticker. $80-85.

Marks on lady head vase #2358. Sticker used 1953-1971.

White bud vase with shades of pink, dark green leaves, and pink rose buds, 5.5", #KW258. $20-25.

White bisque with applied pink roses and blue forget-me-not flowers, 4", #1847W, stamp, sticker. $18-20.

Dainty Miss head vase, 7.5", #7549. (*Courtesy of Mike and Cindy Schneider*) $90-95.

Pair of pineapples, 5.5". There are seventy-two applied pink roses on each of these vases! #KW7283 and stamp is on one, #K7283 and stamp on the other. $75-80 each.

Marks on #7549.

Hand-blown violet glass with white swirls and handle, 7", sticker. $28-32.

Hand-blown cranberry glass with white swirls and handle, 7", sticker. $28-32.

Hand-blown amber glass with white swirls and handle, 7", sticker. $28-32.

Hand-blown cranberry glass with blue swirling lines, 8". $30-35.

Hand-blown orange glass with white swirls, 6.5", sticker. $25-30.

Pair of white vases with gold trim and painted flowers, #427, stamp. $10-12 each.

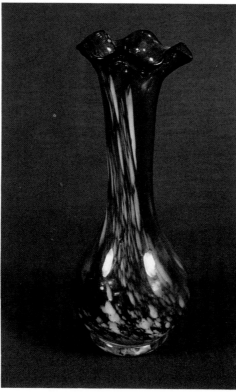

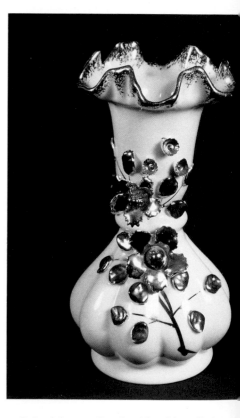

Mark on cranberry vase.

Hand-blown violet glass with white swirls and fluted top, 7.5", sticker. $28-32.

Pale pink vase, fluted, with gold applied flowers and trim, 6", #70435, stamp, sticker. $30-35.

Pink porclain vase with white applied
flowers, green leaves, and gold trim, 6.5",
#191, stamp, sticker. $25-30.

White vase with painted flowers and gold
trim, 6.5", # 03543, stamp, sticker. $18-22.

Pink vase with handle, applied gold flowers
and gold trim, 6", #70435, large red sticker,
stamp. $35-40.

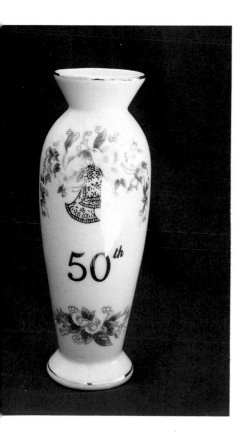

Anniversary vase with green and gray
flowers, gold trim, 6.5", #1102, stamp,
sticker. $15-18.

Marks on vase # 03543. Sticker used 1960-
1983. Stamp used 1955-present.

Marks on vase #70435. Sticker used 1946-
1953. Stamp used 1946-1950.

Wall Hangings

Whether it be a collection of wall pockets, plates, or plaques you are looking for, you will find real beauties made by Lefton China. There are match holders, plant pockets for real or artificial flowers, measuring spoon sets, and plaque groupings for the kitchen. Animal pockets and fish plaques are nice for the den. Or you might want beautifully painted or applied floral plates and plaques for the dining room and framed plaques with Colonial or Provincial women and men, cherubs, and angels for the living or bedroom. Don't forget those sea horses, mermaids, and fish for the bath.

Yellow bird plaques, 5.75" and 2.25", "©Geo Z Lefton," stamp, sticker. (*Courtesy of Mike and Cindy Schneider*) $25-30 pair.

Set of three mermaids, 8.5", 5", 4.5", applied flowers, stickers. $65-70 for set.

Kitchen plaques, 8", #3033, sticker. $10-12 each.

Pair of owl plaques, 8" and 7.75", #4778, stamp, sticker. (*Courtesy of Mike and Cindy Schneider*) $40-45 pair.

White cat plaques, 7.25" and 7", #H548, stamp, sticker. (*Courtesy of Mike and Cindy Schneider*) $40-45 pair.

Pair of Colonial couple plaques, 6.25", #117, stamp. (*Courtesy of Sabra Cummins*) $35-40 pair.

One of a pair, oval, Colonial couple, beige color matte, 8", #KW115B, stamp, sticker. $30-35 for one.

Green "Rock Bass" fish plaque, 7.5", #60420, stamp, sticker. (*Courtesy of Mike and Cindy Schneider*) $20-25.

Fish for the wall, largest is 7", #0419, stamp, sticker. (*Courtesy of Mike and Cindy Schneider*) $28-32 for set.

Pair of horse plaques, 6.5" and 7", #H3321, stamp, sticker. (*Courtesy of Mike and Cindy Schneider*) $35-40 pair.

Blue owl plaque, 8", #4778, large red sticker. $20-25.

Head plaque with five applied pink roses, 8", #1984, sticker. $25-30.

Spice set with six shakers in wood box, 9" high, "©1955 by Geo Z Lefton," large red stickers on each shaker and on box. $75-80.

Chinese wall plaque, black and green, sticker. $18-22.

Praying girl head plaque, 6", #2997, stamp, sticker. *Courtesy of Mike and Cindy Schneider.* $35-40.

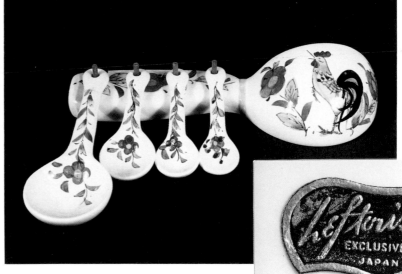

Measuring spoon set with rooster on large half-cup spoon, 8" long. $40-45.

Large red sticker on measuring spoon set. 1946-1953.

Chicken measuring spoon set on 8" long, half-cup spoon, large red sticker, "©Geo Z Lefton." $40-45.

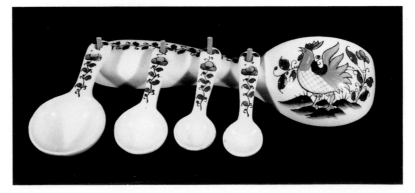

172

This piece is different! Colorful hat with applied bow and pink rose. There are only three leaves but should have been four. The leaf is not broken off, it just isn't there. On the back there are several black X's across the number but has a large red sticker. 6". Perhaps a factory reject. $40-45.

Pair of pitcher and bowl wall pockets, white with orange, yellow, and green, 6", #4368, sticker. $35-40 pair.

Dainty Miss and her friend wall pockets, 6", large red stickers. $150-175 pair.

Colorful kitchen wall pocket, white with painted-on fruit. #2262, sticker. $20-25.

Little girl pocket, 6", #1145, stamp. (*Courtesy of Mike and Cindy Schneider*) $50-60.

Little boy pocket, 6", #1145, stamp. (*Courtesy of Mike and Cindy Schneider*) $50-60.

Bird on a basket pocket, 5", #50410, large red sticker, "Cardinal" on bottom. $25-30.

Little girl pocket with blue ribbon, 5.25", "©Geo Z Lefton," #50275, stamp. (*Courtesy of Mike and Cindy Schneider*) $45-55.

Little girl pocket with pink ribbon, 5.25", "©Geo Z Lefton," #50275, stamp. (*Courtesy of Mike and Cindy Schneider*) $45-55.

Rustic Daisy match box holder, 7", #5402, "©Geo Z Lefton." $25-30.

Black cat pocket with spaghetti fur on cheeks, foot, and tail, rhinestone eyes and gold bow. 5". $30-35.

Mark on black cat pocket.

Boy bluebird pocket, 6.5", #283, "©Geo Z Lefton," stamp, sticker. (*Courtesy of Mike and Cindy Schneider*) $85-95.

Girl bluebird pocket, 6.5", #283, "©Geo Z Lefton," stamp, sticker. (*Courtesy of Mike and Cindy Schneider*) $85-95.

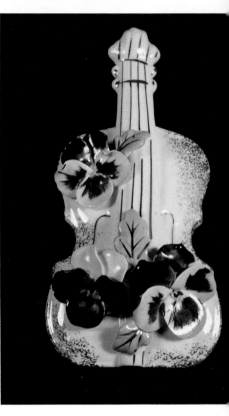

Violin pocket with pansies, 7", #105, sticker. $30-35.

Lord's Prayer pocket with pink and blue forget-me-not flowers, 4", stamp, sticker. $18-22.

Miss Priss pocket, 5.5", #1509, stamp. (*Courtesy of Mike and Cindy Schneider*) $95-105.

Purse pocket with handles and applied rose 5.5", stamp, sticker. $28-32.

Pink cat head pocket with yellow applied bow, 5", sticker. (*Courtesy of Mike and Cindy Schneider*) $45-50.

Brown house wall pocket/planter, 6.5", #H332, sticker. $18-20.

Dainty Miss pocket, 5", "©Geo Z Lefton," #6767. (*Courtesy of Mike and Cindy Schneider*) $90-95.

Little girl in blue dress holding basket, wall pocket, 7", #50264, "©Geo Z Lefton," large red sticker. (*Courtesy of Kim and David Dobyns*) $50-55.

Round white frame with applied branch, pink roses, and leaves, 5.5", #3352N, sticker. $25-30.

Little girl in pink dress holding basket, wall pocket, 7", #50264, "©Geo Z Lefton," large red sticker. (*Courtesy of Kim and David Dobyns*) $50-55.

Plate with applied flowers and leaves, 5", #1178B, sticker. $25-30.

White matte plate with applied bird, flowers, and leaves, 6.5", #KW1017. $30-35.

Plate with bird, stamp, 4". $18-22.

White matte plate with applied wild flowers and gold trim, 6", #4743, stamp, sticker. $25-30.

Mark on back of plate #KW1017.

White milk glass wall plate with fruit, 6", #046, stamp. $18-20.

Gold scalloped-edge white plate with pink and blue flowers, 6", #899, sticker. $22-27.

Colorful plate with painted bird, stamp, 4". $18-22.

Anniversary wall plate, 9.5", #285N, stamp. $20-25.

Fruit plate with scalloped edge and gold trim, 8", stamp. $25-30.

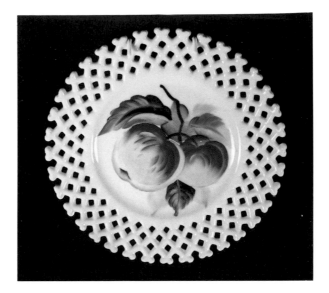

Fruit on lattice milk glass plate, 8", #NE6356, sticker. $25-30.

Pastel green plate with flowers and green leaves, 8", signed "Geo Z Lefton" on front, stamped on back. $30-35.

White milk glass lattice plate with violets, 8", stamp, sticker. $25-30.

Large pink rose on painted, lattice milk glass plate, 8", stamp, sticker. $22-27.

White lattice milk glass plate with floral design, 8", #6350, stamp, sticker. $25-30.

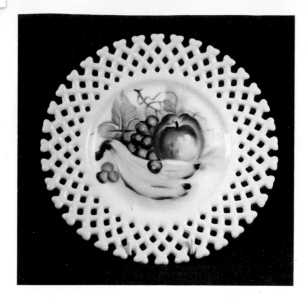

White lattice milk glass plate with fruit design, 8", #6350, stamp, sticker. $25-30.

White violin with applied pink roses and gold trim, 5". $20-22.

Green pear and apple wall pocket, 7", #3848, sticker. $20-25.

Plaque of an angel holding flowers, one of a pair, 5", #KW6417, stamp. $40-45 each.

LAMORE CHINA
ENTIRELY HAND
MADE
G.Z.L. USA
MADE IN
OCCUPIED JAPAN

Marks on white violin. Stamp used 1946-1950.

White plate with applied yellow and blue flowers and gold trim, 9", #669, sticker. $30-35

Plate with applied flowers and bow, 6.5", #KW4374, stamp, sticker. $25-30.

Marks on violin. Stamp used 1946-1953.

Pastel green violin with applied roses and gold trim, 5". $18-20.

Bibliography

DeLozier, Loretta. *Collector's Encyclopedia of Lefton China*. Paducah, Kentucky: Collector's Books, Schroeder Publishing Co., Inc. 1995.

Schneider, Mike. *The Complete Cookie Jar Book*. West Chester, Pennsylvania: Schiffer Publishing, Ltd. 1991.

Deel, Kathleen. *Figural Planters*. West Chester, Pennsylvania: Schiffer Publishing , Ltd. 1996.

DeLozier, Loretta. *Collector's Encyclopedia of Lefton China, Book 2*. Paducah, Kentucky: Collector's Books, Schroeder Publishing Co., Inc. 1997.